AMERICAN INSTITUTE OF CERTIFIED PUBLIC ACCOUNTANTS

Increase Your Personal Marketing Power: Relationship Skills for CPAs

Randi Marie Freidig, CFCS

Issued by the AICPA Management of an Accounting Practice Committee

NOTICE TO READERS

Increase Your Personal Marketing Power: Relationship Skills for CPAs does not represent an official position of the American Institute of Certified Public Accountants, and it is distributed with the understanding that the author and the publisher are not rendering legal, accounting, or other professional services in this publication. If legal advice or other expert assistance is required, the services of a competent professional should be sought.

Copyright © 1997 by
American Institute of Certified Public Accountants, Inc.,
New York, NY 10036-8775

1 2 3 4 5 6 7 8 9 0 PP 9 9 8 7

Library of Congress Cataloging-in-Publication Data
Freidig, Randi Marie.
     Increase your personal marketing power: relationship skills for
CPAs / by Randi Marie Freidig.
     p.   cm.
    "Issued by the Management of an Accounting Practice Committee."
    Includes bibliographical references.
    ISBN 0-87051-183-1
     1. Accounting—Marketing.   2. Accounting firms—Marketing.
3. Businesspeople—Social networks.   4. Business etiquette.
I. American Institute of Certified Public Accountants. Management
of an Accounting Practice Committee.   II. Title.
HF5657.F74   1997
650. 1'3' 088657—dc21
                                            97-4224
                                            CIP

ACKNOWLEDGMENTS

First and foremost my thanks goes to my husband, Dale. His love, support, encouragement, insights, and patience all helped me complete this project. As a CPA, CMC, and former managing partner of both a local and a national CPA firm, he was always there when I needed to bounce ideas around.

I would also like to acknowledge the AICPA, especially Laura Inge, and the Management of an Accounting Practice Committee for having faith in me to produce a book of value. Also, Tracy White and the other CPE directors for allowing me to teach the principles and skills through their state societies. And as important, all the CPAs and CPA firms who have found great value in expanding their people skills—I have enjoyed working with all of you.

My colleagues—Lynn Lively, Robin Ryan, Vanna Novak, Steve Miller, Marilyn Schoeman Dow, and Henriette Klauser—are very important influences to me as a professional speaker and trainer. They have been encouraging me to write this book for years. Richard Schenkar helped with the research.

The biggest surprise was my high school friend, and college roommate, Carole Schmidt. As an English major she used to love correcting my papers. She volunteered to edit my original drafts and this book is much better for it.

The following are members of the AICPA Management of an Accounting Practice Committee Task Force and others who contributed direction, information, and review of this book.

Rick J. Anderson, CPA
Moss-Adams LLP
Seattle, Washington

Louis J. Barbich, CPA
Barbich, Longcrier, Hooper & King
Bakersfield, California

H. Brent Hill, CPA
Rudd & Company
Rexburg, Idaho

Steve Greenberg
Moss-Adams LLP
Seattle, Washington

Lyne P. Manescalchi
Boulay, Heutmaker, Zibell and Co., PLLP
Minneapolis, Minnesota

Nancy Myers
Former Director of Practice Management
AICPA

Judith R. Trepeck, CPA
Trepeck Group
Southfield, Michigan

AICPA Acknowledgments:

Project Editor	Laura E. Inge
Editor	Mary F. Mooney
Book Design	Kim Mangal
Production	Roberta Roberti

TABLE OF CONTENTS

INTRODUCTION

A journey of a thousand miles must
begin with a single step.

— *Chinese proverb*

One of the most important success principles you will ever learn is this: The more people you know and who know you in a favorable way, the more successful you will be in your business or profession. These are the people, and the people they know, who help open the doors of opportunity, give sound advice and contribute input into career and business decisions. They make referrals and introductions, help educate and assimilate information, and, in general, have a positive impact on your value in the marketplace.

This book explores this relationship-building process and its impact on practice development and one's career direction, and answers the following questions. Why do you want to meet new people and stay in touch with others? How do you meet people and make a positive impression consistently? What skills are necessary for building quality relationships? What is the role of trust and integrity in selling yourself, your firm, your services, and your profession? How does all this influence business development?

The process is much more than just collecting business cards right and left, in order to fill your Rolodex®. To build and nurture long-term, mutually beneficial relationships, whether with clients, associates, coworkers, referral sources, or others in the community, you must show a sincere interest in others and have the ability to build rapport and trust.

To put the importance of personal marketing for business development and career success into context, we need to consider what the workplace is like today and what we can expect in the future.

The passage from an agricultural society to an industrial society took thousands of years. The industrial age came and went faster than any other age in history, starting about 1815 and officially ending in the last few years as we entered the information age. The focus has moved from manpower, the use of our *physical* muscles, to mind power, the use of our *mental* muscles.

Today, the main sources of value in the marketplace are knowledge and the ability to tap into and apply that knowledge in a timely and appropriate fashion. Knowledge is power. However, even though we cannot know everything, we can know others who may have the information we need—and vice versa. This helps us be of more service to our clients.

Another change that is affecting the accounting profession has to do with how we approach ongoing business development. Traditionally, most CPA firms have had strong rainmakers, partners whose talent is bringing in business. Most corporations accomplish the same objective by having a sales and marketing department with people dedicated to selling their products or services. Few accounting firms dedicate staff solely to sales and marketing.

Times have changed. Competition for clients is keen. Clients are more fickle. People coming into the accounting field are expected to be more than good technicians. They must also have solid people skills and an entrepreneurial attitude.

Today, every CPA needs to know how to market. Personal marketing skills are needed to land a job, keep that job, and be effective within any organization. Whether by developing business, or keeping yourself and your department visible within the larger organization, you do not want to limit your career. Rather, you want to make yourself indispensable, employable, and very marketable.

You must also master your *people* skills to be effective. Your ability to listen well to clients, ask good questions, uncover your client's needs, and help meet those needs will increase as your knowledge base expands beyond basic accounting principles. By applying your brainpower to the problems and to the needs of the people and situations around you, you increase your value. It will become even more important to read outside your field, become intimately involved in your clients' industries, and be perceived as a partner in their business.

The basic premise of this book is to understand that your most valuable asset is your earning ability and this is tied not only to your technical skills but to your ability to bring in business. The direction of your career will be directly affected by your ability to market yourself and your firm. This book will show you how to evaluate, plan, and execute individual marketing strategies and build interpersonal relationship skills.

Personal marketing skills, like any other skill, require *planned* learning. The first step in the learning process is to recognize the skill and understand why it is important. This *why* gives you a conceptual framework and is covered in chapter 1, "The Value and Importance of Personal Marketing Skills." The next step is to evaluate, plan, and observe a demonstration of how the skills work. The planning and implementation process is addressed in the following chapters:

However, practice makes permanent. So, another important step in the learning process is to make sure we are practicing the right skills in the correct fashion. The specific skills necessary for building long-term, positive relationships are discussed in the following chapters:

Then, we practice, practice, practice. Continual practice establishes a positive pattern, especially if we ask for and get constructive feedback along the way. Since one of the building blocks of effective personal marketing strategies is visibility, chapter 11, "The Value of Visibility," explores ways to increase visibility within your community, specific industries, and your profession. Chapter 12, "Setting Yourself Apart From the Competition," wraps up with reminders on how to set yourself apart from the competition by adding value to your personal and professional relationships...how to be consistently viewed in a positive way by everyone you come in contact with.

Although the process may seem overwhelming to many of you, let me assure you that it can be easy. Just start—and start small. Appendix A, "Sample Worksheet and Personal Marketing Plan," gives you an example of a basic marketing plan. Appendix B, "Partner Level Sample Worksheet and Marketing Plan," gives those of you with many years in the field an idea of how you can increase your effectiveness at practice development. This works with or without the support of your firm and its partners. That's why it is referred to as a *personal* marketing plan. It will influence *your* career success and it is based on what interests *you.*

Quotations are scattered throughout the book. Many of them sum up in a few words what would take paragraphs to explain. Also, key points are highlighted at the end of each chapter.

It is my hope that as you read this book, it will inspire you to step up your learning process as it relates to personal marketing skills. Implementing the ideas in this book will help to ensure lifelong employability. It will also give you the self-confidence to be more social and effective in your networking. The self-assurance you will have because of your proactive approach to your own career and business development will enhance your most valuable asset—your earning ability.

THE VALUE AND IMPORTANCE OF PERSONAL MARKETING SKILLS

"Personal relationships are the fertile soil from which all advancement, all success, all achievement in real life grows."

— *Ben Stein, author*

INTRODUCTION

A partner of a small three-partner firm in the Northwest—I'll call him Tom—went to lunch one day with a banker with whom he makes a point of staying in touch.

During lunch the banker mentioned a customer of his, a foundry owner who was dissatisfied with his CPA firm. Recognizing an opportunity, Tom asked whether he might be able to help. The banker thought so. They talked a little about the foundry business. As they finished their lunch, the banker said he'd get back to Tom about the possibility of meeting with his foundry customer.

Tom went back to his office and immediately did some research. He called a trade association to learn more about the foundry business. He called some of his contacts with experience in the industry. He did some reading on the subject.

The banker called back to set up an appointment for Tom to meet the foundry owner. Once Tom had the name of the owner, he went to work to learn more about him. Through his contacts in the community, Tom found out that the owner is active socially in the community, that he belongs to a golf club and an athletic club, and loves baseball. He has four children. He helps coach a Little League team. He also sits on the board of the Boys and Girls Club and is an active fund-raiser for children's causes.

During the initial meeting with the owner of the foundry, Tom was able to use this information to talk about what interested the owner. He could ask informed questions, bridge conversation, establish rapport, and show his knowledge of the industry and its key issues.

That foundry owner is now one of Tom's clients and has since been a excellent referral source for Tom's firm. Tom and his firm have also referred business back to that banker many times.

This is an excellent example of how personal marketing skills work to build business and enhance a person's career. This CPA has been building relationships and working to maintain them in a positive way over the years. When it was time to do his homework, he was able to quickly tap into his resources.

STRATEGIES AND SKILLS

As you observe CPAs in your firm or community who are successful at bringing in business, you will find diverse styles and approaches. All of them can be equally successful. The difference today, and the one that will persist in the future is that a firm can no longer rely on just a few partners bringing in all the business. It is important to remember that everyone needs to be involved in marketing and selling the firm's services and products.

The more people you know, and who think of you favorably, the higher your value in the marketplace. Therefore, a major strategy for getting ahead in business today lies in the art of developing contacts, maintaining relationships, and tapping into those resources over time. The ability to build strong relationships and effectively manage them can help make your career. These skills also enable you to enhance the success of your organization.

Building a strong network of contacts takes time. Personal marketing skills are necessary to do just that and it also involves strategizing...taking time to plan. It's important to point out the difference between a skill and a strategy, because a skill is not a strategy.

An interesting analogy is the process of taking apart a gun, cleaning it, putting it back together, raising it, and shooting it straight at a target. The process is made up of skills. What to shoot at, when, and where, is a strategy.

Inviting a contact to lunch, handling yourself well at the table, moving easily from social to business conversation, comfortably asking for a referral, following up appropriately, and keeping track of the effort are skills. Knowing who to invite to lunch, when, how often, and for which reasons, involves strategy.

A strategy for career success entails meeting people, making connections, and building resources deliberately and in a formalized fashion.

CONNECTIONS, RESOURCES, PEOPLE, NETWORKS

Personal marketing skills can be defined as those skills that assist a person in comfortably and confidently making contacts, building and maintaining relationships, and using this dynamic professional network to assist in his or her career. This kind of marketing influences the people and organizations an individual works for, as well as their customers and clients. Personal marketing is also referred to as *relationship selling*—selling oneself and one's services to others.

Networking is the term used today to describe this active process of building and managing productive relationships. This process takes in everyone you work with, including the following:

- Peers
- Managers
- Supervisors
- Partners
- Department heads
- Team members
- Administrative staff

It also includes everyone within and between the following organizational units:

- Departments
- Teams
- Locations
- Subsidiaries
- Divisions
- Functions
- Offices

It also includes the external relationships with the following:

- Clients
- Suppliers
- Referral sources
- The community
- Customers
- Vendors
- Competitors

We have long known that human beings strive for a sense of belonging. Research is also being reported in the business press about the advantages of these personal and professional relationships. Wayne Baker, in his book *Networking Smart*,[1] provides the following examples of the benefits of the good managing of business relationships:

- Managers with large personal networks get higher paying positions than managers with small networks.
- Managers with large, well-diversified networks get promoted faster and at younger ages compared with their peers with underdeveloped networks.
- Professionals who find jobs through personal contacts (instead of classified advertisements or other impersonal means) find better, more permanent satisfying jobs.
- Building good working relationships is the main reason for success of managers who take charge of a new situation.
- Close relationships with customers save money. It costs three to five times as much to get a new customer as it does to keep an old one.
- Strong partnerships with reliable suppliers yield lower costs and higher quality products and services.

Business effectiveness, in general, depends more on human-related activities, such as building relationships, interpersonal skills, and communication, than on technical skills and abilities.

---

[1] Wayne Baker. *Networking Smart.* New York: McGraw-Hill, Inc., 1994.

There are, of course, many more reasons and advantages to developing a strong network of friends, colleagues, and resources than just for business development and career success. We need to recognize the vast power this strong, deep network of relationships and put it to positive, constructive use.

The cumulative effect of your marketing effort creates recognition and name familiarity, reinforces an image or reputation, and puts your name or the firm's name in potential buyers' minds. If you examine how a potential client might hear about your company, you will find many different modes of communication, some intentional and some coincidental. (See figure 1-1.)

FIGURE 1-1: HOW CLIENTS HEAR ABOUT YOUR FIRM

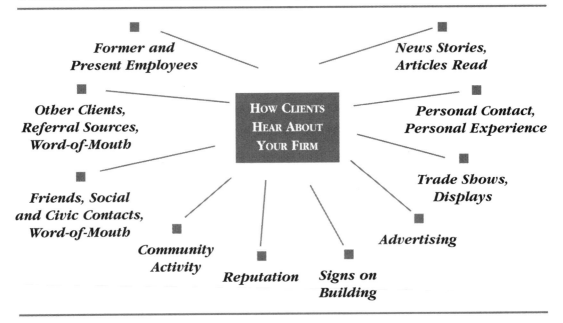

Personal marketing skills also include those that keep you and your name out there in the community. Those of you who work for large firms need to create visibility for yourself within the organization. This may not be as critical in smaller firms; however, it is also astute to make sure people know you and see their experience with you as positive.

Adele Scheele, in her book, *Skills for Success*, describes hardworking employees as either *sustainers* or *achievers*.[2] Sustainers are the employees who wait to be noticed. Achievers, on the other hand, are the ones who make sure people—the right people—know what and how they are doing. They are willing to toot their own horn. Sustainers are often just as qualified and experienced, but feel uncomfortable about promoting themselves. They are, therefore, often overlooked for promotions, special projects, and other work-related rewards. Self-promotion is a necessary activity for professionals with any kind of career goals.

In the same way that clients get information about your organization, the business community also learns about you from various sources. (See figure 1-2.)

FIGURE 1-2: HOW OTHERS HEAR ABOUT YOU

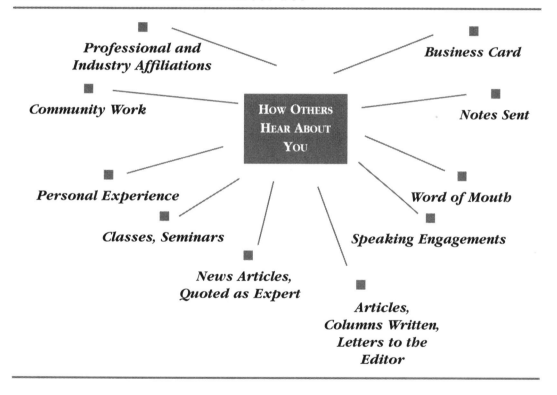

Professional and Industry Affiliations

Business Card

Community Work

Notes Sent

HOW OTHERS HEAR ABOUT YOU

Personal Experience

Word of Mouth

Classes, Seminars

Speaking Engagements

News Articles, Quoted as Expert

Articles, Columns Written, Letters to the Editor

---

[2] Adele Scheele. *Skills for Success*. New York: Ballantine Books, 1981.

Although networking has always been a critical business skill, its importance in today's changing job market cannot be underestimated. All the changes in the public and private sectors, such as downsizing, right-sizing, restructuring, home offices, telecommuting, entrepreneurial endeavors, team approaches, partnering, and globalization, only add to the importance of building a strong network. No matter where you go or what you do, that network is mobile. It travels with you!

KNOWING VERSUS DOING

Having knowledge about something is one thing. Being able to use that knowledge is something else. Competence is having the skill to apply what we know. Knowing the value of building and nurturing long-term business relationships is a start. Most of us stumble on making time and building the skills that make us comfortable and self-assured about networking. It does not have to be difficult. To become part of your career strategy, it does need to be planned, and it means putting yourself out there, taking risks.

It means that when you go to an association meeting or industry function, you make a point of sitting with and getting to know new people. It means that when your firm puts on an informational seminar to which clients, potential clients, and referral sources are invited, every effort is made to welcome, connect, and follow-up with each individual attending. It means using your business card as it is meant to be used— as a physical reminder of you, part of your marketing effort.

The importance of these actions is reemphasized throughout this book. Each activity is not hard. It just needs to be implemented.

MARKETING VERSUS SELLING

People often get confused as to what is considered *marketing* and what is *selling*. An easy way to distinguish between the two is that marketing is getting your name, your products, and your services in front of potential buyers. Selling, then, is getting that potential buyer to buy. There will always be a need for some selling. But the aim of marketing is to make selling superfluous. The aim of marketing is to know and understand the client so well that the service fits him or her and sells itself.

The Marketing Advantage,[3] published by the AICPA, has a good explanation of the difference between marketing and selling as it relates to the CPA practice.

---

[3] *The Marketing Advantage.* Colette Nassutti, Ed. New York: AICPA, 1994, pp 3–4.

Marketing includes the full range of activities that create awareness of your firm, foster a positive image, and elicit the interest of desirable prospects. It encompasses all aspects of strategic planning, including research, analysis, and setting business goals for the firm. Marketing also includes the planning and execution of promotional activities, such as advertising, media relations, and direct mail. Because marketing activities tend to be strategic in nature, they are usually planned and executed by the firm as a whole or at least by its management.

Personal marketing then would be the full range of activities used to create awareness of you as a commodity in the marketplace. You want to foster a positive image and elicit others' interest in you, your skills, and your services.

The Marketing Advantage defines *selling* as beginning where marketing leaves off. "That is, it encompasses all of the activities required to convert qualified prospects into satisfied clients. Here, the effort involved usually centers around a series of face-to-face encounters between one or more members of your firm and a prospective client."

Personal marketing focuses on awareness and building relationships. Ultimately, we want to build a strong, dynamic network of contacts who—

- Know our name, company, and how to reach us.
- Know what it is we do and can explain it to others.
- Have faith in our ability to deliver and serve them and those they refer.
- Know what kind of customers and clients we want and will readily refer them to us.
- Know what kind of information we need and will be willing to help find it or provide it.

The flip side of dynamic relationships is that we offer the same benefits to others. It is often a matter of asking a favor and expecting to return it at some future date. In order for this give-and-take atmosphere to be effective, a person has to have a genuine interest in others and be willing to help out whenever possible. Others are a resource for you, but you must in turn be a resource for others. It is a two-way street.

FOUR PHASES OF PERSONAL MARKETING

Personal marketing skills build like other skills. With conscious effort, you can get better and better at marketing yourself, your business, and your profession. We all tend to go through four phases as we develop personal marketing skills to enhance career and business goals.

Phase One—Building a Professional Image and Reputation

This phase usually begins while you're in college and continues after your licensing and in the early years on the job. It's during this phase, while you're building competencies and gaining technical experience, that you begin to build professional relationships.

At this time, it is important to get involved in professional organizations such as your state society, industry associations, and the Jaycees. It is also advisable to join and get involved in community nonprofit, religious, or political organizations. Some very important things happen in these organizations because they are a safe learning environment that allows you to grow. By volunteering for projects, heading committees, and otherwise actively participating, you will be given opportunities that might not otherwise be available to you to gain and build skills such as public speaking.

At the same time, others within your industry, market, community, or profession are given the opportunity to observe you in a relatively risk-free environment. They have the opportunity to experience you in a "giving" mode. They can observe how you perform tasks and how you follow through on commitments, as well as your team spirit and ability to influence others. Your character and integrity take shape in the business community. This first phase is doubly important because while you are building your image and reputation, personal contacts are established.

Phase Two—Developing Relationships

Your character, integrity, and credibility become consistent and well known in this phase. The people you met earlier will have also moved along their career paths. They will have evolved into solid contacts and resources.

Here, rather than just meeting new people, you also take time to develop those relationships. You cultivate your social interactive and interpersonal communication skills. These skills are used with people within your firm, and within the industries in which you are developing an expertise. This second phase is important because developing long-term relationships results in potential buyers.

Phase Three—Practicing Effective Selling Skills

This is the phase most people shy away from either by rationalizing that they are not born salespeople, or by delegating to others. Nevertheless, everyone needs to know how to sell—their products and services, their ideas, themselves.

Phase three is very important. It is at this time that your reputation and effective selling skills shine and, as you practice effective selling skills, sales increase. You understand and communicate that you are not selling tax services or audits, but rather expertise and peace of mind. That expertise is offered to clients who may be using services in one area but may not know about your expertise in other areas. You feel comfortable asking for referrals from satisfied clients, their bankers, lawyers, and other professionals that have benefitted from the quality of your work.

Personal marketing is the only way to consistently increase business. And, in order to be effective, you must also know what it takes to sell larger value services and products. Those are products and services that cannot be understood on the first go-around.

Phase Four—Maintaining Client Relationships

It is well documented that keeping an established client is less costly than getting a new one. Nevertheless, we put more time and money into wooing a new client (the *courting* stage), than we do after the sale (the *marriage* stage).

In this phase, keeping clients requires strong interpersonal skills and a keen interest in others and their businesses. It means taking clients (or bankers, lawyers, and other referral sources) to lunch, calling occasionally to inquire about their business, to ask how they are doing, what they are thinking, and to find out about their concerns and frustrations. Offering information, networking clients, partnering in their business success—all this is part of maintaining and nurturing a relationship.

The importance of this phase cannot be overemphasized. Nurturing and maintaining client relationships results in repeat business, expanded services, and referrals.

PLANT NOW, HARVEST LATER

We are all familiar with the principle that you must sow in order to reap. It makes no sense to go out to your garden to pick tomatoes if you never planted any. Or to plant tomato seeds on the first of August and expect tomatoes on the fifteenth.

This principle is the basis for business development. The contacts you make now and the relationships you build and nurture will eventually reap business and career opportunities. In our wishful thinking, we would like opportunity, in the form of business, to simply appear, even though we know better. In order to get clients, we must *do* something. That something is building a strong professional and personal network. And it takes time.

As we grow professionally, our network grows as well. It takes time, patience, diligence, and an understanding of the work involved. It is well worth it, professionally and personally.

■ ■ ■

Keep the following in mind when approaching personal marketing skills.

■ Building positive relationships is an ongoing process.

■ Take time to plan and set work-related goals.

■ Relationships are built on mutual trust and respect.

■ The more people you know, the more value you bring to the marketplace.

■ Knowing and doing are two very different things.

■ Taking the time and making the effort to meet people and stay in touch involves both strategies and skills.

■ Ask for the business.

■ Take advantage of opportunities as they present themselves.

TAKING

OWNERSHIP

*"If I could wish for my life to be
perfect, it would be tempting, but I
would decline, for life would no
longer teach me anything."*

—*Allyson Jones, writer*

INTRODUCTION

To understand the advantages of taking ownership, one only has to observe experienced sailors. With a specific destination or goal in mind, and the belief they are responsible for getting to their destination, they use their skills to maneuver the rudder, sails, and engine to reach that destination. All the time, they are having to adjust to change—change in the wind, tide, and currents. Good sailors are proactive. They do not see themselves as victims of the climate or weather. Rather, they expect and prepare for these changes. They take responsibility for their results.

In today's business climate, it is important to take ownership for business development as well as for the direction of your career. You must manage your career with specific goals in mind and acknowledge responsibility for the results. Without direction and a sense of ownership, you will find yourself feeling frustrated and lacking enthusiasm.

Today, a sense of ownership is essential for success in both your career and business development. In order to move forward and improve at what you do, it is important to know where you are now and where you want to go in the future. Not only must you have a sense of direction, but you must be proactive in getting there. Personal marketing is key, otherwise you become discouraged, and overwhelmed by the feeling that you have wasted time and not taken advantage of opportunities.

Personal marketing skills, like any other skill, can be developed and mastered. However, some people seem to have a natural predisposition for liking and getting along with others. Some people are gregarious by nature. Others function much better one-on-one. Some people establish rapport easily. For others, it takes a conscious effort. No matter where you are in the spectrum, there is always room for improvement. In the learning process, we instinctively know that we—

- Must identify behaviors and actions attributed to a skill.
- Must engage in consistent practice to gain new skills.
- Must take small incremental steps rather than big leaps.
- Prefer to practice and learn the skill in privacy whenever possible, to avoid embarrassing ourselves in front of peers.

Too often, marketing focuses tightly on strategic planning and fails to include an assessment of the skills needed to implement the strategy. Which skills and competencies you want to build depends on your business development strategies and career goals. Self-assessment is a valuable tool to help plan, monitor, adjust, and evaluate progress.

Sir Isaac Newton's law of cause and effect states, "To every action, there is always opposed an equal reaction." It is a universal, fundamental truth. It means that every cause (action) will create an effect (reaction) approximately equal in intensity. Making good use of our minds, skills, and talents will bring positive rewards in our lives. It takes personal responsibility, however, to make the best use of our talents and time in order to result in personal and professional gains.

More of the same brings more of the same—this is not a smart strategy in today's competitive marketplace, not if you want to progress. As much as any growth business, an individual setting career goals and planning strategies needs to look at strengths, weaknesses, opportunities, and threats (SWOT). It does not matter where you are in your career—it is just as important for the new graduate as it is for someone ten years short of retirement.

STRENGTHS AND WEAKNESSES

If you are serious about improving your skills, you need to know what you already do well and what you need to improve. Assessing the skills needed to reach career and business goals is as important as assessing the skills you need to improve in anything. For instance, as a golfer, my whole game could improve. However, if I examine my game as it is today, the best use of my practice time should be to concentrate on working with my putter and my wedge. By isolating a small number of areas, I can focus my practice time. Specific drills and exercises will help improve my putting and the accuracy of my wedge. With time, patience, and perseverance, that part of my golf game should improve.

Assessing the skills that need improvement is the first step to meeting goals or strategies. Although I do not aspire to go on a pro tour, I do want a 15 handicap; right now, it is 19. When I first started playing golf, my goals were to golf under 105 and to hit the ball straight, and not necessarily very far. With those goals, hitting a bucket or two of golf balls at the driving range helped. The more I learn about the game, the more drills I do with a bucket of balls.

Building skills starts with the basics, the foundation on which to improve. By analyzing your strengths and weaknesses, you will be able to identify interests and competencies. Both affect how you do your work and whether or not you enjoy it. Both will affect your success at implementing a personal marketing plan. Assuming you have career and business development goals (to be discussed further in chapter 4, "Developing a Personal Marketing Plan"), ask yourself the following questions. What are your strengths and weaknesses? Are you clear about where you want to go and what you want to accomplish? What are your interests? Are you self-disciplined? Are you focused? Do you have a positive, upbeat attitude? Are you socially skilled?

Do you like people? Do you find it easy to be with others? Do you follow through? Do you update your technical skills beyond what is required? Do you get excited about learning? Are you motivated? Do you see yourself as a partner with your clients? Are you service-oriented? Do you have an entrepreneurial attitude?

OPPORTUNITIES AND THREATS

In advising a client, you might ask the following question: "What is the greatest threat to your business success?" If a client were to answer, "I don't know," you would very likely point out that the answer itself holds the greatest danger—but also the greatest opportunity.

The same advice applies to you, as you ask yourself where you want your career to go, or how much business you want to be responsible for bringing in. Not knowing may be the most likely cause of your failure, or it may be the source of your best opportunities.

Do you enjoy writing? Public speaking? Do you like meeting people? Do you know how to sell? What opportunities exist to enhance your career and increase the amount of business you could bring in? Which areas of accounting do you like? Dislike? Discovering opportunities and threats and analyzing their impact is not an easy task. It is, however, very illuminating and also critical if you are serious about your career.

If you have mentors in the office or within your industry, ask them for feedback. Others will recognize strengths and weaknesses in you that you may not be able to identify on your own. The same is true for opportunities and threats. Some people are very visionary and forward-thinking. They may be able to help you see where trends are headed, or be able to explain the goals of the firm in relationship to your advancement. Reading outside your field will broaden your ability to forecast both opportunities and threats.

The following questionnaire, exhibit 2-1, is an approach to doing a self-assessment. Answer yes or no to each of the questions. You should be able to look at every *no* and get a sense of where your weaknesses are and whether or not they are a threat or an opportunity.

EXHIBIT 2-1: EVALUATION TOOL—PERSONAL QUESTIONNAIRE

Yes *No*

Professional Growth

☐ ☐   I take pride in my technical skills.

☐ ☐   I willingly take on more responsibility.

☐ ☐   I am proud of my profession.

☐ ☐   I feel I contribute to my career.

☐ ☐   I enjoy learning.

☐ ☐   I am proud of my firm.

☐ ☐   I see our firm growing and being more successful.

☐ ☐   I feel I can make a difference with my firm.

☐ ☐   I understand all the services my firm offers.

☐ ☐   I feel good about my coworkers.

☐ ☐   I seek feedback.

☐ ☐   I look for ways to improve systems, procedures, and processes.

☐ ☐   I consider myself good at selling skills.

☐ ☐   I make time for public relations activities such as volunteering, writing, and public speaking.

☐ ☐   I am active and building a positive reputation in industry associations.

☐ ☐   I maintain an enthusiastic attitude toward marketing training and the enhancement of my sales and marketing skills.

Client Relations

☐ ☐   I understand the unique business issues of my clients and uncover and anticipate client needs.

☐ ☐   I see myself as partnering with my clients to ensure their success.

☐ ☐   I make the client feel like their company's well-being is uppermost in my mind.

☐ ☐   I devote extra time each month to learning more about my clients' business, industry, and special challenges.

☐ ☐   I often ask clients how I am doing, and what I could be doing differently.

☐ ☐   I provide work in a timely manner.

☐ ☐   I keep the client apprised of the progress of the engagement.

☐ ☐   I return all client calls within two hours.

Yes No

☐ ☐ I resolve all problems as completely as possible and in a timely manner.

☐ ☐ I always look for ways to exceed client expectations.

☐ ☐ I can talk with a broad range of client personnel about issues of interest or relevance to them.

☐ ☐ I have a good working relationship with my clients.

☐ ☐ I acknowledge clients' personal special occasions such as birthdays, anniversaries, and honors.

Interpersonal Relationship Skills

☐ ☐ I am a good listener.

☐ ☐ I am comfortable in social situations.

☐ ☐ I enjoy socializing with clients and associates.

☐ ☐ I am comfortable meeting new people.

☐ ☐ I consider myself a good host and am comfortable hosting others.

☐ ☐ I know what is expected of me when I am a guest.

☐ ☐ I write thank-you and acknowledgment notes regularly.

☐ ☐ I enjoy talking with people about a wide array of subjects.

☐ ☐ I can be both persuasive and informative when speaking.

☐ ☐ I find people extremely interesting.

☐ ☐ I make people feel valued and important.

☐ ☐ I invite younger staff members to join me at events such as association meetings, civic club meetings, and client entertainment functions.

From time to time, jot down strengths, weaknesses, threats, and opportunities as you think of them. You might use a chart such as the following one, exhibit 2-2, "Evaluation Tool—Tracking SWOT," or use sheets of paper in a notebook. The idea is to capture your thoughts and analysis about your SWOT in order to prepare yourself for a successful future.

EXHIBIT 2-2: EVALUATION TOOL—TRACKING SWOT

SWOT	Affecting My Career Success	Affecting Business Development	Part of Current Career Goals
STRENGTHS			
WEAKNESSES			
OPPORTUNITIES			
THREATS			

RELATING TO OTHERS

Personality testing is another assessment that is helpful in getting along with others. Of the many versions available, some are self-administered and analyzed, and others involve computer or third-party analysis. Myers-Briggs and Performax are two well-known testing instruments. The advantage of these instruments is that they help us understand human behavior and therefore help us improve our people skills by being more flexible, understanding, and respectful of others' behaviors.

Basically, these instruments help identify communication styles. Understanding the various styles can help you be more persuasive. They can help you work well with other people's natures rather than against them. Over the centuries, thinkers have divided the human race into personality styles. Many of the systems are adapted from the work of psychologist Carl Jung. Each of us, it seems, has a preferred way of approaching people, tasks, and time.

Adapting occasionally to another's communication style or blending styles can yield impressive results. Say, for example, you are about to present a proposal to a new client. The way in which you present it depends on the client's communication style. If the client's style is controlling and dominant, then you do not want to start off with a long description of problems and solutions, with in-depth explanations of procedures, as you might if the client's dominant style was analytical. Rather, you might recap their goals and spell out your solutions, giving the timeline and costs involved.

By using a variety of communication styles, you learn to speak to others in their own language. It is especially effective if you manage or supervise others. In fact, many companies now use testing instruments before hiring because communication is critical in the workplace. Examining differences in behavior and learning to adapt to them allows you to perform at optimum effectiveness and build alliances with your associates.

If you have never experienced even the most basic quadrant-based personality testing, you are in for a treat. It will provide many insights and answers into why people do not do things the way you do. It is well worth the time and effort to go through the tests. People will never look the same to you.

A good book on this subject is titled *The Platinum Rule*.[4] It is based on the premise that you should do unto others as they would like done unto them. The book offers two effective tools. First is the principle of treating others as they would like to be treated, which sensitizes you to the differences among people. The second tool is the examination and explanation of the four basic personality types and how to put this knowledge to use when working with people.

This knowledge will help you feel more comfortable about calling clients just to touch base, because you are equipped to communicate in the way that is meaningful to them. It will influence your ability to influence and persuade others to action. It is one more piece of the puzzle as it relates to communication.

THE "ME, INC." ATTITUDE

One night, early in my career, I came home from a dinner meeting of my local professional association. When my husband, Dale, asked me how it had gone, I launched into a description of the dry, tasteless chicken dinner, and said that if the food did not improve, I would drop my membership. I will never forget my husband's reaction. He looked at me and said, "Randi, you weren't there for the food. You were there to invest in your future." He added that no one should care about my career more than I do.

---

[4] Tony Alessandra, PhD, and Michael J. O'Connor, PhD. *The Platinum Rule*. New York: Warner Books, Inc., 1996.

21

He was right. That association meeting was just one opportunity to meet people and build professional relationships—to say nothing of the educational aspects of membership. In fact, the idea for a business that I later started came to me with the help of someone I met through the association.

That conversation with my husband was the beginning of my realization that my career was of my own making. It was my first acquaintance with the concept of being CEO of "Me, Inc.," which means thinking like an entrepreneur when it comes to one's own career goals and objectives. It means taking ownership.

If each of us thinks of ourselves as CEO of a small service company called "Me, Inc.," then our attitude shifts to being proactive. In order for any business to be successful, it takes more than a good product or service. Someone has to want (buy) the product or service. The goal of successful businesses is to get and keep customers profitably.

As CEO of "Me, Inc.," you must have a vision by which to set your goals and allocate resources to ensure your viability in the marketplace. Like any successful business, there are several activities you must engage in to insure your service is competitive and profitable. Think of these as your departments.

1. *Production.* This activity focuses on fulfilling your contract with your current employer—doing what you were hired to do and creating the value your client expects.

2. *Sales and Marketing.* The following activities fall into this department, and they focus on your personal marketing skills.
    a. You want to create visibility within your department, company, profession and community.
    b. Self-promotion activities, such as writing articles, calling clients and resources to maintain contact, are necessary.
    c. Building a strong network of resources will impact your value in the marketplace.

3. *Human Resources and Personnel.* The function of this department is to measure your performance (what is expected of you), and to seek out and provide training to sharpen and expand your skills.

4. *Finance.* Here is where you evaluate and invest in yourself wisely. For your time and money, and that of the firm, you want a good return on your investments. Every class you attend, every book you read, or every conference you go to should be evaluated against your overall career and business goals, weighing the time and costs involved.

5. *Research and Development.* This function is becoming increasingly important as the job market changes and as our clients become

more fickle. It relates both to your career and the work you do for your current employer. Earlier in this chapter, we explored the value of self-assessment. With a clear understanding of SWOT as it relates to your career, you can then develop strategies to stay current and marketable. The same applies to your current position. You will want to develop strategies around this same kind of information for your department, team, or office location.

6. *Administration.* This involves the function of developing systems to record your progress, including CPE requirements, other certification, how you capture contacts, keep in touch, awards, community involvement, and keeping your resume current. (You should update your resume every six months. Why? Doing so will give you a good idea as to whether you are making progress or not.)

No one should care more about your career than you. That does not mean that the current organization you work for will not support your development in many ways. It does mean, however, that in the last analysis, your professional growth and development is your own responsibility.

Many organizations are introducing entrepreneurial thinking to their employees. The purpose is to encourage employees to think, as they work with clients, about how to expand work and service opportunities. The effort is about identifying opportunities, isolating problems, and offering creative solutions. The more you understand about running a successful business, the more successful you will be in partnering with your clients. People who think like entrepreneurs think differently than those who think like technicians. Technicians usually do not know how to run a business, therefore do not pursue opportunities for adding value to client services.

RAINMAKING FOR THE NEXT CENTURY

Consistent business development involves specific competencies. We need to examine what has worked in the past and how it can work today. The key is to see yourself as a *relationship manager.*

The Hay Group, an international consulting firm headquartered in Arlington, Virginia, identified twenty competencies that predict success in professional and managerial jobs. Relationship-building competencies are one of the twenty competencies identified.[5] Specifically, these refer to the ability to establish and maintain strong, positive relationships with

---

[5] Lyle Spencer, Jr., PhD, Signs Spencer, and David McClelland, PhD. *Competency Assessment Methods: History & State of Art* (referred to as "the little green book"). Arlington, VA: HayMcBer, The Hay Group, 1994.

a wide range of people over time. A job competency is defined by the Hay Group as what outstanding performers do more often, in more situations, and with better results than average performers within a specific organization. This is why some people are referred to as the rainmakers in the firm. They are outstanding performers when it comes to demonstrating the skills needed to bring in business.

In order to increase your relationship-building skills, it helps to analyze which skills are demonstrated by outstanding performers. Not only can they showcase their knowledge and competence, but these superior performers seem to have an underlying motive to succeed. Your attitudes, values, and self-image will affect your success. You want to learn what makes them *think* the way they do. Find role models or mentors who fit this description and interview them. Talk to them about what they think in certain circumstances and how they act.

Because relationship-building skills are so important, they will be examined further in chapter 6, "Essential Skills for Building Quality Business Relationships."

■ ■ ■

Keep the following in mind when taking a proactive stance with your career.

■ You need to know where you are in order to plan where you want to go.

■ Discover your individual comfort level and formulate an approach to enhancing relationship-building skills in your own unique way.

■ Adopt the attitude of an entrepreneurial thinker.

■ See yourself as a relationship manager.

■ Observe the successful and do what they do.

■ Learn more about personality styles to improve your communication with others.

■ Be proactive with your career.

■ Take time to analyze your strengths, weaknesses, opportunities, and threats.

■ Focus on what you enjoy doing, while giving other interests a chance to develop.

CONDUCTING A SELF-ASSESSMENT

*"Everyone has talent. What is rare is
to recognize it and then have the
courage to follow the talent to the
unknown places where it might lead."*

—*Sandra Day O'Connor,
Supreme Court Justice*

INTRODUCTION

As we saw in chapter 2, "Taking Ownership," in order to move forward and improve at what you do, it is important to know where you are now and where you want to go in the future. Self-assessment is a valuable tool to help plan, monitor, adjust, and evaluate progress. This chapter will help you evaluate your network of contacts.

Your success as a business professional depends as much on who you know as what you know. The value you bring to your job, your clients, and your organization is directly related to the depth and breadth of your Rolodex® . . . who you know and who knows you in a positive light.

Cultivating a dynamic network begins at home in your youth and continues throughout life.

A dynamic network can be defined as all of the following:

- An association of individuals, companies, or other entities
- A broad and diverse range of relationships
- Established and potential relationships
- A mutual benefit to all involved
- A source of assistance, support, and the exchange of information and knowledge
- Like-minded individuals who join forces to share business opportunities and clients
- Formal and informal relationships

The process of building and maintaining relationships with people who are or might someday be useful in achieving personal and professional goals is *networking*. Networking, which involves both strategies and skills, is all of the following:

- A process of identifying and developing relationships with people who can add value to your organization
- A strategy to develop pathways to opportunities
- A business strategy of giving, sharing, and receiving information
- An opportunity to compare services and products
- A way to engage others in getting your job done
- A way to help others in getting their jobs done
- An opportunity to help others pursue their career goals
- A process that continuously improves

ASSESSING CURRENT CONTACTS AND RESOURCES

Most people are pleasantly surprised by the number of people they actually know personally. If you evaluate the people you currently know, and factor in the people they know, the potential size of your network is mind-boggling. Your circle of influence, as shown in figure 3-1, is like the ripples created by a pebble tossed in the water ... the circle becomes larger and larger.

FIGURE 3-1: YOUR CIRCLE OF INFLUENCE

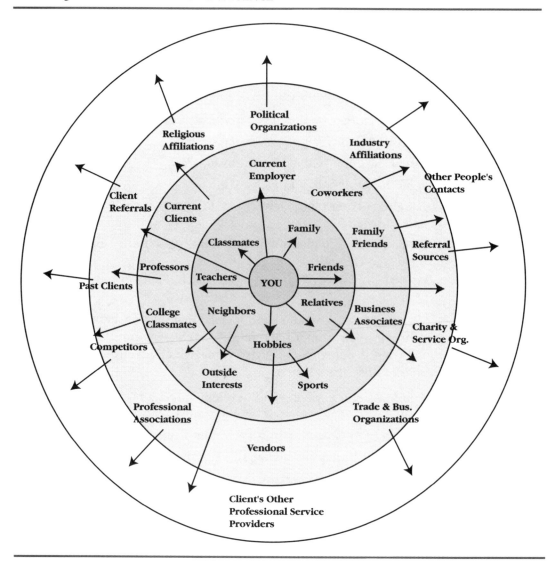

Sheer numbers, however, do not make for an effective and dynamic network. It is the kind and quality of the experience and the relationship that makes things happen. Your network provides you with the following:

- Friendships
- Business associates who can refer business
- Job opportunities
- Access to information you may not otherwise have
- Access to sources of knowledge
- Introductions and access to influentials
- Opportunities to help and be a resource to others
- Recognition as a expert with an industry or profession
- Inspiration to learn, grow, take risks, and try new things

The following list recaps the sources of your contacts.

- Family and Friends
- Political Organizations
- Trade and Business Organizations
- Clients
- Past Clients and Customers
- Current and Past Jobs
- Friends
- Professional Associations
- Charitable and Service Organizations
- Client Referrals
- Competitors' Clients
- Outside Interests and Hobbies
- Religious Organizations
- Industry Affiliations
- School or College Classmates and Teachers and Professors
- Client's Banker or Lawyer
- Professional Associates
- Other People's Contacts

The first step is to analyze your current, active network and your current personal marketing activities. Then determine where you need to spend more time and with whom in order to build stronger professional relationships to reach your goals.

Current Involvement in Organizations

Exhibit 3-1 is a tool designed to help you evaluate your involvement in organizations. Knowing where you currently spend your time will help in the evaluation of your personal marketing efforts. With this information, you will be able to make better career decisions.

List all the professional, trade, business, industry, civic, nonprofit, and personal organizations you belong to. The personal ones include athletic clubs, private clubs, religious and political organizations, school, day care, and children's activities, such as soccer leagues.

Next, make a note about how active you are. Do you go to meetings regularly, sign up for committees, or get involved in special projects?

For each group, estimate how many meetings, scheduled or otherwise, you attended for that organization within the last year. List the roles or activities you got involved with. Did you chair a committee? Get a table of colleagues and associates together for a fund-raiser? Sit on a panel? Write for the newsletter?

The last column addresses the issue of your willingness to take a risk—to put yourself out there. Do you sit with people you already know? Do you sit with coworkers instead of making a point of meeting new people?

EXHIBIT 3-1: EVALUATION TOOL—CURRENT INVOLVEMENT IN ORGANIZATIONS

List Organizations (List Each One)	Rate Your Activity Level: (A=Active and Involved; M=Member in Name Only)	Number of Events or Meetings Attended This Past Year	Roles Filled, Volunteer Activities (List)	Do I Go Out of My Way to Meet New People Here? (Yes/No)
PROFESSIONAL				
INDUSTRY OR NICHE				
COMMUNITY OR CIVIC				
PERSONAL				

Current Client Contact

Exhibit 3-2 is a tool that will help evaluate how much time you spend getting to know clients and their other service providers. It will give you an idea of who you currently spend your time with in nonbillable activities, such as "doing lunch," golfing, theater, and other outings. You will find this analysis to be a rich source for business development.

First, list all your clients. If you are just getting into the business, list the ones you are working on. If you have been in the business for years, list the top 20 percent of your clients as defined by your firm's criteria.

List the name of your primary contact(s) within the client organization. Write down the number of contacts you have had with them this year. Do the same for your client's attorneys, bankers, and other service providers.

Depending on where you are in your career, you will probably see some distinct patterns here. Perhaps you only know the controllers, not the owners. Maybe out of fifty clients, you personally know four of their bankers, eight attorneys, and one insurer. In which law firms and banks do you know the most people? This activity will help you see who you will need to know. Ask one of the shareholders to help. They can contact their banker resource and ask whether that banker would introduce you to one or two of the younger bankers in their organizations so you can begin building professional relationships.

EXHIBIT 3-2: EVALUATION TOOL—CURRENT CLIENT CONTACTS

Nonbillable Meetings and Contacts

List Clients and Companies	Contact Name and Relationship	Client's Attorney and Firm	Client's Banker and Bank Name	Client's Insurer and Company Name	Client's Other Service Providers: Names and Companies

Contact With Current Business Associates

Exhibit 3-3 is a tool that helps evaluate your current business associates who are not clients or associated with clients. These are the people who most likely are (or will be) in a position to refer business, act as a resource, and/or benefit from your referrals. These are the people you want to know and have know you.

List your top three industries based on client work or interests. Again, identify your contacts. How often do you keep in touch? Have you referred business to each other? Do you know the executive director of the trade association? Which banks are a rich source of business contacts? Have you developed a relationship with the person who sells benefits packages?

EXHIBIT 3-3: EVALUATION TOOL—CURRENT BUSINESS ASSOCIATES

Professional Associates	*Names of Contact(s) I Know Personally*	*Number of Contacts With This Person in the Last Year and Date of Last Contact*	*Business Referred: (T = They Have Referred Business to Me; I = I Have Referred Business to Them)*
INDUSTRY OR NICHE (*List the top three*)			
BANKS			
LAW FIRMS			
INSURANCE COMPANIES			
OTHER SERVICE PROVIDERS			

This next tool, exhibit 3-4, takes a close look at your public relations and personal marketing activities. Some of this will be a crossover from exhibit 3-1, "Evaluation Tool—Current Involvement in Organizations." You want to look at what you are currently doing to create visibility and to build trust and credibility.

Look at each activity, how often you did it, and which markets it affected. I also think it is a good idea to start identifying what you enjoy doing today. If you are very skilled at a task, such as public speaking, but do not enjoy it, that should influence future planning. However, if your skill level is low, with practice you may find that your enjoyment level goes up as well.

From the analysis and examination of these four tools, you will get an idea of your strengths and weaknesses as they relate to contacts and resources. What you do with the information will depend on your career and business development goals and objectives. The following are examples.

1. If your goal is to move up within your organization and become partner, ask yourself the following questions. Who do you need to know? Who needs to be aware of you and your work? Who could coach and mentor you? Who can help you strategize visibility?

2. If you have developed an interest in a particular industry, and would like the challenge of serving that marketplace, do you have access to the experts who can refer business and/or recommend you? Who are the other professionals serving this market (such as insurers, bankers, and lawyers)? Who are the major suppliers and vendors? Who are the leaders in the trade associations? Who writes about the industry?

3. If you are interested in making a name for yourself within your profession, how active are you in the accounting associations? Who do you know who could coach you? Do you have access to the influentials and experts? Do you know key CPAs who can complement the services offered by your firm?

The sample worksheets given in exhibits 3-5 and 3-6 are intended to help you develop a personal marketing plan that fits your current situation, helps your firm retain and grow its client base, and enhances career development. There are a number of questions to be answered, and from those answers, some goals and action should become obvious. The worksheets are best used in your work with a coach or mentor. See appendixes A and B for completed examples of the worksheet shown in exhibits 3-5 and 3-6 as well as marketing plans.

EXHIBIT 3-4: EVALUATION TOOL—CURRENT PERSONAL MARKETING ACTIVITIES

Activity	*Number of Times I Did This, This Year*	*Market That This Activity Affected*	*My Enjoyment Level (1 to 5 Scale)*	*My Skill Level (1 to 5 Scale)*
Give speeches				
Teach classes or give seminars				
Write or publish articles				
Be quoted or cited as an expert source by the media				
Sit on a board (public or civic service)				
Head or serve on committees				
Send thank-you and acknowledgment notes				
Maintain a database for contacts and clients				
Other				

EXHIBIT 3-5: SAMPLE WORKSHEET FOR DEVELOPING A PERSONAL MARKETING PLAN

1. Where are you now in your professional development? If your firm has position descriptions, which one best describes your current situation?

2. What could you be doing that would help those senior to you better serve existing clients?

3. Which industries do you really enjoy?

4. In which area of technical expertise do you want to become more proficient?

5. How effective are you at—
   Speaking in front of a group?
   Conducting meetings?
   Listening?
   Writing?
   Delegation?
   Consensus building?
   Selling or persuading?
   Personally presenting a professional image?
   Entertaining and hosting?
   Staying in touch with people?

6. How did you help the firm last year—
   Retain business?
   Cross-sell services?
   Add new clients?
   Increase the referral base?
   Create a larger awareness of the firm?

7. How would you describe the position you want to have within the firm in the next three years?

8. What do you think your chances are of achieving that position?

9. What do you think the firm needs to do to help you?

EXHIBIT 3-6: SAMPLE WORKSHEET FOR DEVELOPING A PERSONAL MARKETING PLAN AT THE PARTNER OR SHAREHOLDER LEVEL

1. Where are you now in your professional development? If your firm has position descriptions, which one best describes your current situation?

2. What could you be doing that would help those you supervise better serve existing clients?

3. Which industries do you really enjoy?

4. In which areas of technical expertise are you an expert?

5. Are there areas of technical expertise in which you want to be known for your expertise?

6. How effective are you at—

    Speaking in front of a group?

    Conducting meetings?

    Listening?

    Writing?

    Delegation?

    Coaching?

    Consensus building?

    Selling or persuading?

    Personally presenting a professional image?

    Entertaining and hosting?

    Staying in touch with clients and referral sources?

7. How did you help the firm last year—

    Retain business?

    Cross-sell services?

    Add new clients?

    Increase the referral base?

    Create a larger awareness of the firm?

(continued)

8. How would you describe the position or role you want to have within the firm in the next two or three years?

9. What do you think your chances are of achieving that position or role?

10. What do you think the firm needs to do to help you?

These questions and others relating to how you will go about assembling and building your network to help meet work-related goals are addressed in chapter 4, "Developing a Personal Marketing Plan."

■■■

Keep the following in mind when evaluating your network relationships.

■ What goes around, comes around. Give first. Ask if you can be of help.

■ People want to know what's in it for them, even friends, clients, and associates.

■ Find ways to stay in touch. Do not overlook using E-mail and the Internet.

■ Do not worry if a contact fails to reciprocate immediately...the timing might be off.

■ Be patient. Plant now, harvest later.

■ Do not burn bridges.

■ Constantly work at expanding your network.

■ Focus on your primary networks.

■ Introduce your best business associates to each other.

■ First of all, pay attention to clients you already have. They are a great source of expanded services and referrals.

■ Relationships need to be dynamic to work—give and take, back and forth.

■ Influentials listen to recommendations of other influentials—word of mouth is important.

Developing a Personal Marketing Plan

"All you need is the plan,
the road map, and the courage
to press on to your destination."

—*Earl Nightingale, motivational writer*

INTRODUCTION

No matter where you are in your career—whether you are a staff accountant, a manager, or a partner—the many demands on your time mean that planning your personal marketing is an essential part of effective career and business development. Even an informal marketing plan will help you use your time wisely.

This chapter presents an approach that can be followed to develop a personal marketing plan. It starts out with having a current career objective. The next step involves the evaluation of who you now know and which organizations you are involved in. With that information in hand, it is more obvious who you need to know, and which skills and activities you need to accomplish your objectives. Developing a specific plan will lay out how you'll go about this. (See appendixes A and B for examples of completed personal marketing plans.)

Planning focuses your personal marketing strategy. You will know who to spend time with, who you want to keep in touch with on a regular basis, who you need introductions to, which organizations to join, which committees and boards to be active on, and how all this fits into your career goals and your firm's overall business development goals. You probably do not have the time or interest to do it all. Planning strategically gives you a higher return on your investment.

CURRENT CAREER OBJECTIVES

No two accountants within the same firm will necessarily have the same career objectives. This is the area that is specific to the likes and dislikes and aspirations of each individual. Although two CPAs may both want to become managers, and then partners, their areas of interest within the public accounting industry can vary.

Which position within the firm do you hold now, and which position do you want to hold in two to three years? A senior accountant responsible for preparing tax returns and financial statements may desire to be a manager in two years. Because of individual interests, this CPA may want to eventually specialize in estate and tax planning.

A CPA who is currently a partner also needs to explore career goals. Which position do you hold, or which role do you have now? How can you continue to hold it and increase its value to the firm? Or, if there's another position you want to hold or expertise you want to be known for, how will you go about attaining it?

Chapter 3, "Conducting a Self-Assessment," addressed assessing your current network of contacts and activities. Let's take a closer look at how to expand your network and how that fits in with your personal marketing plan. The evaluation tools (exhibits 3-1 through 3-6) presented in chapter 3, give you a sense of your strengths and weaknesses within each of the following four categories:

1. Your profession, including the following:
   - Professional associations
   - Other CPAs
   - Media

2. Your niche or industries, including the following:
   - Industry and trade associations
   - Business organizations
   - Experts and influentials
   - Clients, present and past
   - Client referrals
   - Clients' other service providers
   - Your competitors' clients
   - Targeted prospects
   - Media

3. The community, including the following:
   - Civic organizations
   - Service organizations
   - Charitable organizations
   - Influentials
   - Political organizations

4. Your personal professional circle, including the following:
   - Other service providers
   - School affiliations
   - Hobbies and outside interests
   - Religious organizations

Go back to the exhibits in chapter 3. Exhibits 3-2, "Current Client Contact," and 3-3, "Current Business Associates," give you a sense of who you currently know and where you are lacking contacts. Exhibits 3-1, "Current Involvement in Organizations," and 3-4, "Current Personal Marketing Activities," tell you how involved you currently are in your profession and community.

Those of you at the partner or shareholder level have a more complex network and will want to consider the following questions:

- Which contacts have the most influence over the client's or prospect's behavior?
- Which contacts within a client organization have the greatest influence over the buying decisions?
- Which contacts are the most influential within an industry or segment?

The point is to identify *who* you need to know and *where* you can find them. You will want to target certain people, industries, organizations, and activities to maximize your marketing efforts. To capture this information, use exhibit 4-1, "Identifying Contacts."

EXHIBIT 4-1: IDENTIFYING CONTACTS

Contacts

Who	Company or Organization	Industry or Niche	Connection to My Goals	Date of Contact

This information can be placed in a three-ring binder with the other evaluation tools and your goals and can also be computerized with timed reminders.

Another important step is to evaluate the value of the contact and activity to your career development and to the firm's practice development. This involves two key areas—your career goals and your firm's goals—which are examined in the following sections.

Your Career Goals

You are developing your ability to cultivate your role as a respected leader in both your firm and the community. If you are aspiring to develop or expand your expertise in an area of interest or a niche market, or interested in leadership positions within professional and trade organizations, this will influence who you decide to target. Your career goals, however, should mesh with your current firm's business development goals, and never be at their expense.

Your Firm's Goals

It is important to understand your firm's goals. Several issues surface here. First, what kind of clients and/or industries meet the firm's targeted client profile? Second, where does your current new business come from? Third, do all the shareholders support the marketing goals? Often, there is general consensus but little consensus on the specifics.

Let's start with the current new business sources. Every firm should have a system to capture data on where business is coming from. It might be as simple as a line on a form, or a more formal questionnaire. If your firm captures this information, your job will be easier. The bottom line is that you need to know who is referring you to new clients.

One CPA firm analyzed their sources of new business as follows:

- 28 percent from social and civic friends
- 24 percent from internal growth by present clients
- 21 percent from current clients referring others
- 14 percent from lawyers
- 6 percent from bankers
- 7 percent from others including past clients, other CPAs, former employees of clients

This kind of analysis helps you in several ways. It tells you which relationships are critical to your firm's business development. It reminds you to nurture these relationships on a regular basis. It may give you an idea as to where you need to spend more time developing referral sources and strategic alliances. It reinforces the value of being actively involved in your community and with business associates.

For example, several research projects have revealed startling facts about getting referrals from clients.[6,7] As many as 95 percent of the clients interviewed say they would refer if asked. As few as 20 percent of the clients were ever asked for referrals by their CPA. A valuable part of your personal marketing skills is the ability to ask for referrals confidently and comfortably.

Another interesting fact was uncovered by David Maister, who is possibly the premier student of professional service firms.[8] He recently surveyed partners of several firms by asking them to assign their clients to one of three categories that can be described as follows:

1. "I like these people and their industry interests me."
2. "I can tolerate these people and their business is OK—neither fascinating nor boring."
3. "I'm too professional to ever say this to them, but, honestly, they are not my kind of people and I have no interest in their industry."

Those surveyed put about 30 percent of their clients into the "like" category, 50 percent into "tolerate," and 20 percent into "don't care for them." Maister was appalled. Why, he wondered, spend the majority of your time with clients who don't do much for you? What is his advice? Reject lousy business.

The value of understanding which industries and businesses your firm targets and why makes prospecting easier. You have a clear idea of the profile of a good client. Some clients are more profitable than others. Some are more fun.

Another part of the equation is to identify the best opportunities for winning new clients before launching into your marketing efforts. Since the market for accounting and tax services is extensive, most firms divide the marketplace into discrete groups of potential clients, based on geography, industry, meeting client needs, competition, specializations, and so on. With this information, the firm's growth strategy will focus on the following.

---

[6] Weaver and Tidwell, L.L.P. Fort Worth, TX.

[7] Jay Nisberg. "Ask and You Shall Receive Referrals." *CPA Marketing Report.* January 1996.

[8] David Maister. "Are You Having Fun Yet?" *The American Lawyer.* June 1994.

1. Sell more current services to existing clients.
2. Sell existing services to new clients.
3. Develop new products and services to sell to existing clients.
4. Diversify by developing new products and services that can be used to win new clients.

By knowing how your firm plans to grow through client, market, and product or service development, you can tailor your personal marketing efforts to those of the firm. It works best as a team effort.

Any organization, in order to be successful today, must have a game plan. Team sports provide an appropriate analogy here. In order to be a winning team and have a successful sports organization, it takes commitment to a clearly defined game plan. The team players need to buy into the plan and its timetable, and coaches need to lead the team and inspire the players to give a 100-percent effort.

It is unrealistic to think that the staff can get excited about and participate in marketing activities if partners do not participate. The challenge today, then, is to create a culture within the firm in which marketing is encouraged by the coaches and accepted by the players. It is this team spirit that reinforces the importance of marketing and makes it happen.

If your firm has a concrete marketing plan, it will be easier for you to see how your personal plan fits in. It will also be easier to get support from the partners and others in the firm.

If your firm lacks a formal marketing plan, schedule time with the managing partner, administrative partner, or the person assigned the task of overseeing the marketing aspect of the businesses. Review your plan with the following in mind.

1. Determine the kind of client the firm is looking for:
   - Profit to firm
   - Expertise and interest to partners
   - Size

2. Identify quality referral sources:
   - Clients
   - Industry and community influentials
   - Professional services associates

3. Identify industry or niche interests and expertise:
   - Where your interest and expertise lies
   - Others within the firm
   - Prospects and resources

4. Evaluate client satisfaction, retention, and value-added services.
   - Methods to keep them happy and loyal
   - Where services can be expanded
5. Create professional development opportunities.
   - Occasions and activities for visibility
   - Interpersonal communication skills
   - Job-related nontechnical skills (problem solving, decision making, selling)

Once you have an idea of how your personal marketing plan fits in with your firm's plan, it will be easier to get your marketing projects off the ground. You want and need support for your goals and objectives.

THE VALUE OF MENTORS

A few words need to be said here about the value of mentors. Benjamin Franklin once said, "There are two ways to acquire wisdom; you can either buy it or borrow it. By buying it, you pay full price in terms of time and cost to learn the lessons you need to learn. By borrowing it, you go to those men and women who have already paid the price to learn the lessons and get their wisdom from them."

This is the essence of mentor-mentee relationships. By going to CPAs who are ahead of you in their career, and by opening yourself up to their input, advice, and guidance, you can save yourself the time and thousands of dollars of learning costs that would be incurred if you learned by yourself.

Your choice of mentors will ultimately help determine the person you become and the things you achieve. The larger the firm, the more important mentors become in career development. A mentor can help you learn the corporate culture, politics, how CPAs traditionally move up within your firm, who you need to know within the firm and within specific industries, and where you can most effectively spend your time.

Characteristics of a Mentor

The mentors you choose should be people you respect, admire, and want to emulate. The advice you seek should be the following:

- Guidance regarding your character and people skills
- Specific ideas on how you can do your job better and faster
- Guidance and options regarding career advancement within the firm
- Advice and direction for your personal marketing goals

You will want to choose a mentor within your firm. This person might be at a different location, in a different city, depending on the size of your organization. You also might look for mentors within the community or within an industry. These role models can give you different perspectives.

Working With a Mentor

Like any other relationship, this one needs to be nurtured as well. To keep your relationship with your mentor on healthy ground, do not overlook the following.

- Work, study, and practice continually to get better and better at what you do. The very best mentors are only interested in helping you if they feel it is going to be of value to you.

- Set up appointments with your mentor and stick to the time allotment. Mentors are also very busy with their own work and lives, and are not receptive to anyone who wants to take up a lot of their time.

- Have clearly defined goals and objectives that you plan to review with your mentor. Your mentor cannot give advice unless he or she knows what you want to accomplish.

- After each meeting, drop your mentor a short note telling him or her about your progress and about what you are doing. Also express your gratitude and appreciation for his or her time and advice.

- Review your progress and direction annually. Find a way to personally thank your mentor for his or her guidance.

The fastest way for you to succeed is with the good advice and counsel of men and women who have spent years learning how to succeed in the accounting profession. If you do this on a regular and systematic basis, you will open up doors of opportunity and possibilities for you that today you cannot even imagine.

DEVELOP AN ACTION PLAN: SET GOALS

At this point you have an idea of *who* you need to target and *which* organizations you need to be active in. Now you need to decide *how* you will accomplish this. The magic of goal setting cannot be overlooked. It helps bring things into focus and provides deadlines.

Do not forget to be SMART with your goals, as shown in the following:

S = **Specific**

M = **Measurable**

A = **Attainable**

R = **Relevant**

T = **Timely**

For the most effect, set one-year and three-to-five-year goals. Your three-to-five-year goals give you the bigger picture. Short-term goals allow you to devise a specific plan of action. Consider the following example.

Three-to-five-year goals are to—

- Be viewed as an expert in the restaurant and manufacturing industries.
- Serve as a state officer in a trade association.
- Bring in a specific number of dollars in new business from this industry or thirty new clients (ten per year).
- Be promoted to a manager by year three.

The one-year plan of action is to—

- "Do lunch" with an industry person (twenty contacts).
- Meet key suppliers of industry clients (list by name).
- "Do lunch" with someone in your primary network (twenty contacts).
- Write three acknowledgment or thank-you notes weekly (50 x 3 = 150 contacts).
- Subscribe to and read trade magazines (list).
- Write and publish one article for the trade.

These goals might seem very realistic to one person and overwhelming to another. However, superior performers take goal setting seriously. After assessing the strengths and weaknesses in your network, bank on the strengths and manage the weaknesses. For example, you may have a strong relationship with the owner of a restaurant chain. Develop that relationship further by getting to know the owner's other service providers. Ask for referrals. And refer business to that client.

You may also find that you need to spend time getting to know the president or owner of your client company as well as you know the controller or CFO. If you do not have strong relationships with the owners, presidents, and CEOs, then filling that gap is something on which to focus.

Another area for goal setting focuses on the other service providers your clients use. Do you personally know your clients' bankers, lawyers, insurance brokers, or even their computer consultants? Every banker has clients and they too are looking to expand their business. Getting to know these other service professionals can be mutually beneficial.

Remember that your personal marketing plan should address several areas that encompass your professional development and the firm's business development: getting visibility through public speaking and writing, community and industry involvement, professional skill development, client services, cross-selling, referral sources, and targeting. Once your plan is in place, it will take action on your part to make it come alive. Chapter 5, "Working the Plan," addresses how to work your plan effectively.

■ ■ ■

Keep the following in mind when developing your personal marketing plan.

■ Goal setting means putting goals and objectives down on paper.

■ A plan of action represents the steps needed to meet your goals.

■ Putting your plan of action into motion takes time management, discipline, and focus.

■ Break bigger goals into small, manageable pieces.

■ It is the process of getting from one point to another, rather than the goal itself, that is often the most rewarding and fun.

■ Give activities a chance. It takes time.

■ Not all clients need to fit the target profile.

■ Sometimes we choose to take on a new client because we like the people, the business, or the change of pace.

■ If you plan to write articles, get input on how to best showcase your own expertise as well as that of the firm.

■ Look for opportunities to accompany the more experienced CPAs in your firm on client calls or when they meet with referral sources.

■ Mentors and role models are invaluable...they can reduce the learning curve.

■ Ask for feedback from those you respect.

■ Do not give up. Persevere.

■ Be willing to try another activity or approach if the first fails.

WORKING
THE PLAN

*"The majority of people meet with
failure because of their lack of
persistence in creating new plans to
take the place of those which failed."*

— *Napoleon Hill, author*

INTRODUCTION

All the analysis of the strengths and weaknesses of your network will be lost if you do not work your plan. Knowing and doing are not the same. One addresses increased awareness; the other concerns behavior. If you want to build skills, it involves changing behaviors—changing the way you currently do or do not do things.

Remember, personal marketing skills involve creating visibility, meeting people—the right people—keeping track of them, building positive long-term relationships, interacting with these contacts to help meet work-related goals, and nurturing the relationships.

Now that you have formed ideas about who you need to know, which activities you need to be involved in, and how these tie into your goals and the firm's objectives for business development, you are ready to work the plan.

EXPANDING YOUR NETWORK

A big part of the personal marketing plan you developed in chapter 4, "Developing a Personal Marketing Plan," focuses on developing and expanding an effective professional network. At the very least, you will want to regularly ask yourself the following questions:

- Is my list of contacts within my company or organization growing monthly?
- Is my list of contacts within my area of interest (industry niche) growing monthly?
- Is my list of contacts within my profession growing monthly?
- Is my list of contacts within the community growing monthly?

If you answered no to any or all of these questions, you have an indication of where you need to focus. People tend to make marketing harder than it needs to be. If you stay in touch with a different person weekly, that is fifty contacts in a year (assuming you take two weeks for vacation). Calling or corresponding with one person each day of the fifty weeks adds up to two hundred fifty connections a year. Since most of us eat lunch every day, why not make it a point to target resources—for referrals, expertise, assistance or business—as luncheon companions.

If you "do lunch" even as infrequently as twice a month, and contact someone by phone or mail each week, it will make a huge difference. Success comes from the *doing*, putting your plan into action.

If a firm could get all its partners to go out to lunch with clients and referral sources on a regular basis, that firm would have all the business it could handle. This activity gives partners (or you) the opportunity to touch base, learn more about the needs of the contact (and how you might be of help), ask for referrals, and in general, build rapport. This is what outstanding performers do to build strong alliances. Be determined not to be lazy about it, and you will be developing a positive habit and a very effective one at that.

RECORDING PROGRESS

By setting specific, measurable goals, you can then mark your progress. If you have contact management software, this is easy to track. If not, set up a notebook with weekly pages. An example for the "people" or "who to meet" part of your plan might look like the example shown in exhibit 5-1.

EXHIBIT 5-1: WEEKLY CONTACT WORKSHEET FOR BUILDING AND MAINTAINING CONTACTS

	Weekly Contacts		Week of_____	
Person/Company/ Phone Number	*Connection to Marketing Plan*	*Purpose*	*Results*	*Next Contact or Follow-up*

By using exhibit 5-1 or a similar contact worksheet every week, you can easily record your progress. It also helps establish positive habits. Most CPAs do not take advantage of tax season, even though it is a good time to spend extra time with existing clients. Businesspeople's focus tends to be financial in nature during this period, even though this can be an advantageous time to cross-sell services, ask for referrals, and in general, add value to the existing relationship.

You will also want to track the activities you identified in your marketing plan. Exhibit 5-2, "Marketing Plan Activities Time Line," is an example of how this might be accomplished.

EXHIBIT 5-2: MARKETING PLAN ACTIVITIES TIME LINE

Marketing Plan Objective	Specific Activity	Action Taken to Date	Projected Completion Date	Date Accomplished	Results Realized

Managing your network of contacts helps you manage your time better, be more effective, and allows you to record and evaluate your results. The following sections address the how, who, and what of tracking your contacts and your networking activities.

How

The first challenge is deciding how you will track your network of contacts. Whether you use a Rolodex® file, a notebook, or software designed to manage the myriad tasks for staying in touch, your system needs to be logically organized and easy to access.

The following are some of the various systems you can use to track contacts.

White Card System

Either 3x5 or 4x6 cards are used to keep basic information on each person. Business cards, if you have them, can be attached. The advantage of this system is portability. You can carry clean cards with you at all times and fill them out as you meet people. This keeps your impressions and any details of any given individual, his or her interests, concerns, and so on, fresh and handy. If you meet with a person in the future, the card can go along with you to refresh your memory beforehand. Using this system in conjunction with software gives you maximum coverage.

Rolodex® System

This system of keeping people's business cards in an organized file has been around forever. To be effective, however, include more information than that printed on a person's business card. This can be accomplished by using a Rolodex® that takes large cards. Business cards can be attached, and extra information can be written down much as you would with the white card system.

These two systems are easy to use, but there are disadvantages. Neither holds an enormous amount of information about the contacts. It is hard to build and track a marketing effort with them.

Contact Management Software

First used by telemarketers and others in sales, software is fast becoming the norm for everyone who wants to maintain and nurture relationships. Most software options have a database, word processor, activity schedulers, report generators, and business forms. They make it easy to add contacts, and schedule and track activities, from meetings to mailings. Other features include network support, E-mail integration, group management capabilities, calendar and address book printing, and automatic dialing. Information can be automatically exchanged between portable and desktop computers to keep files and data current. The value lies in the automated action plan, which is more than a "to do" or "wish" list.

The kind you use will depend on the following:

■ Whether or not it ties into the firm's database

■ How you will be using it

■ Whether it goes with you when you leave the firm

Two underlying objectives inform the choice of software. First, you want your own personal and professional network to be portable. Your contacts and resources are part of the value you bring with you from one workplace to the next.

At the same time, however, it is critical for any firm to have a system that is available for all staff to use, access, and update. An effective sales and contact management system is immeasurably valuable for the firm's client service, business development, and marketing. Better service results if the firm can stay in constant touch with clients by providing them with timely information throughout the year. A good system also facilitates the planning and implementation of marketing precisely targeted at current, past, and potential clients. The firm can also prospect for information by tracking client activity.

For instance, within seconds you—or anyone in the firm—should be able to identify the following. Which prospects have been sent the firm brochures? Which have had a personal contact and by whom? Who in the firm is assigned to a particular engagement? When was the last time someone talked to the client? Have they received the latest changes to the pension plan laws? Who should be invited to a specific informational seminar?

Who

Now let's address the question of *who* you keep in your network of contacts. We all receive dozens of business cards as we network, mingle, and move through the workday. Which ones are important to keep and which should be tossed? Part of this question will be based on how sophisticated your contact management system is.

Even the simplest system, such as a Rolodex® file, should be cross-referenced. Sometimes you may not recall a person's name, but you will remember his or her company. Or vice versa. Do you organize by business, industry, geographic location, interests, where you met the person, educational background, and so on?

Let me suggest the following basics to remember when meeting new people.

1. Ask for a business card, if appropriate.

2. Always date the card, note the place or event at which you met the person, and any reminders such as interests, physical attributes, or something you promised (for example, a call, article, or the name of one of your resources).

3. Rate the person as an A, B, or C in one or more of the following categories:
   - Sales lead (business development)
   - Resource or referral source
   - Good connection (in your niche, industry, community)
   - Interesting (hobbies, skills, interests)

If you do no more than this, those business cards floating around your desk and in your drawers will assume more value. Then, when you have time, you will know to follow up with the "A" contacts first. Taking the time to evaluate these new contacts also reinforces how important people in your network can be.

Now let's address the people you already know—clients, past clients, referral sources, associates, industry or niche influentials, and community leaders. Without question they belong in your data file. Besides basic business information you keep on clients, there is a lot more you will want to know—the more personal side rather than the business information. This personal information helps you humanize your marketing strategy.

What

There are many advantages in capturing information about your clients and others. The more detailed information you have about a person and his or her organization, the more focused you can be about meeting that individual's needs. A well-developed database will—

- Allow you and your firm to focus on what interests the client the most.
- Give others in the firm a way to come up to speed quickly.
- Become the foundation for building long-term relationships.

By noting preferences, such as when someone prefers to take calls, which restaurants he or she likes most, favorite charities or sports, you gain the advantage of using that information to focus on what interests that individual.

Harvey Mackay, in his book *Swim With the Sharks Without Being Eaten Alive* (New York: William Morrow & Co., 1988), outlines a system his company has used for years. It is the Mackay 66, a customer profile with 66 questions that is completed by his sales staff over time. In addition to the usual business information, it also contains information about the customer's personal chemistry and characteristics, motivation, and idiosyncracies. This information puts the company in a better position to understand the customer's traits and creatively market to them.

The idea is to give yourself an advantage in the marketplace by really knowing your client. The Mackay 66 covers the customer's education, family, business and career background, special interests, lifestyle, and insights into how he or she does business. For a complete list, refer to Mackay's book. At the very least, however, you want to be acquainted with the following:

- Nickname or the name the customer prefers to be called (and correct spelling!)
- Birth date and city or place of birth
- Spouse's name and birthday
- Anniversary date
- Children's names and ages
- Family interests
- College, honors, degrees, and extracurricular activities (sports, teams, fraternity or sorority)
- Military service
- Professional and trade association activities
- Community and civic activities and interests
- Favorite charities
- Offices held or honors
- Status symbols in office
- Ties to home or schools
- Smoker or not; drinker or not
- Favorite restaurants and foods
- Favorite vacations and destinations

And this is just the beginning. In a ninety-minute lunch, you can learn everything from the size of someone's home to his or her golf handicap, from views on the state of education to favorite vacation spots, from hobbies to family dynamics. You are not playing a new version of Trivial Pursuit. Rather, you are establishing yourself as a good listener. If you go back to the office and make a note of the client's upcoming vacation, you can review those notes before the next call. If you ask how the vacation was, or how his or her daughter's soccer tournament turned out, the client will be impressed that you remembered.

This is important if you are discussing expanded services, a downturn in the economy, or a financial statement. If you are perceived as a good listener, the chances are much better of working out problems and addressing sticky issues.

The personal touch has a lasting impact on building long-term relationships. People are flattered and impressed. The goal is to pay attention to the person across the table, to make him or her feel valued. How to use this information will be examined later in this chapter.

EVALUATING THE EFFECTIVENESS OF CONTACTS

This ties back to the last chapter in which you developed a marketing plan. You want to know who is referring business to you, how often, and whether these referrals meet the target client profiles for the firm. Not all clients and referral sources are the same.

An evaluation will give you an idea as to whether or not you are getting referrals from your clients. If not, why not? As reported earlier, it may be attributable to the fact that you are not asking for referrals on a consistent basis.

The importance of knowing the effectiveness of your contacts as it relates to your career development and the firm's business development is that you want to target those who are the most helpful. One of the biggest errors in networking and nurturing contacts is the failure to pay enough attention to existing clients and proven referral sources.

YOUR FIRM'S NETWORK IS VALUABLE

One of the most valuable assets of any firm is its network of contacts and resources. Some form of network—however informal—exists within every firm. Making the best use of this source can start with building your awareness of it. Pave the way to understanding and developing your firm's network by creating a forum to identify it. Every participant in the forum has, over time, built relationships with key referral sources. Rather than ferret out attorneys or bankers on your own, ask for assistance. The goal is to turn an informal network into a resourceful, formal one. As people grow and gain experience in the firm, it is in the firm's best interest to give managers and staff accountants access to expertise, systems, information, technology, geographic coverage, and other resources they cannot otherwise personally command on their own.

CULTIVATING AND NURTURING RELATIONSHIPS

The relationships you develop with clients, referral sources, alliances, and others in the community must be maintained and nurtured. A graphic analogy that paints a picture of how contact management works is to think of an irrigation system. Suppose you raise vegetables. Each vegetable has unique requirements for soil, fertilizer, water, pest control, sunlight, and the growing season. No responsible farmer or, for that matter, anyone with even the smallest pea patch expects to water, fertilize, and harvest all the plants in the same fashion and on the same timetable. If you program the irrigation system, all the variables are taken into account and the water and fertilizer are adjusted accordingly.

You and I need to approach our clients and contacts with the same scrutiny. Not all clients need the same kind of attention or personal contact. You might think of your marketing strategy as an irrigation system that sustains your client contact. This takes planning and follow-through.

The sales and marketing industry recently reported research that documents the importance of this nurturing if your product or service cannot be understood on the first go-around (like a car wash or dry cleaning). The research found that before 1977 you could sell with between four and six contacts. In 1990, it took from four to nine contacts. By 1992, it was up to nine to twelve contacts. Today, it is estimated to take twelve to fifteen contacts with a prospect to produce enough time, trust, and need in order to convert a targeted prospect to a client.

Since few of us have the time to meet face-to-face with prospects, let alone clients, that many times, our marketing strategy becomes critical. Only some of these contacts will be face-to-face or on the telephone. Others will be the following:

- Firm brochures and marketing pieces
- Direct mail and advertising
- Media exposure
- Articles you have written or in which you were quoted as a resource
- Newsletters
- Position or issue-related papers
- Speeches and classes
- Word of mouth
- E-mail, Internet, and World Wide Web
- Personal experiences with you

As you can see, the advantages of having all this computerized will make your life much easier. You want to spend your time effectively and be more efficient when you use the telephone, meet someone for breakfast or lunch, or invite people to an event. It also underlines the importance of having a coordinated marketing plan with the firm.

If you write an article (or use someone else's) on the challenges of succession planning for closely held companies, why not send it out to all your clients and professional associates that would be interested in this topic? With a solid database, you can do this and record who received it and when.

PUTTING YOUR NETWORK TO WORK

It is one thing to have a strong network. It is quite another to be able to tap into it for referrals and leads, or to build alliances, or to add value for existing clients.

The First-Things-First Approach

You need to know which services your firm offers, who the firm expert is and, if needed, who outside the firm can be accessed for their expertise. You need to know all the particulars about current and targeted clients as these data relate to business development, profitability, and firm growth.

You need to know which services are currently being used by your clients, and what opportunity exists to expand services and add value. You need to pinpoint the most effective sources of referrals and lead generation.

If your firm has this information, the task becomes much easier. If your firm lacks this kind of information, you might want to suggest implementing a system to capture it.

For the most part, your personal marketing plan needs to be easy to implement. If it is not, the chances of your success are nil. Try not to make the plan any more complicated than it needs to be. You might use the following approach:

1. Using the chart in exhibit 5–3, identify the services you and your firm offer, who the experts are in your firm, and those areas that call for outside expertise.

   This approach will give you an idea for alliances with outside experts. More importantly, it is a reminder of all the services you currently can offer clients. If you meet with clients, you gain an idea of the direction to take for conversation and questions.

2. Using the chart in exhibit 5-4, identify, by client, which services are currently offered and which services could be offered. This evaluation helps target clients you can talk to about expanding services. You can keep it in your client file as a reminder.

3. Identify clients and associates you want as referral or lead generators. By identifying your key referral sources, you can make sure you stay in contact with them in a meaningful way. It is also a reminder of the importance of asking for referrals from clients.

EXHIBIT 5-3: IDENTIFY SERVICES AND EXPERTS

The Firm's Services and Experts

Services	Offered: Yes or No	Firm Expert
Audit Services		
Audited Retirement or Health or Welfare Plan		
Bankruptcy		
Benefits Consultation		
Bookkeeping and Accounting Services		
Business Consulting		
Business Expansion		
Business Valuations		
Cash Flow Analysis and Budgeting		
Computer Consulting		
Debt Refinancing		
Debt Share Reorganization		
Estate and Retirement Planning		
Financial Planning		
Forecasts and Financing		
Information Brokering		
Internal Control Review		
Inventory		
Litigation Support Services		
Management Advisory Services		
On-line Access for Tax, Accounting and Management, Research Libraries		
Payroll and Sales Tax Reviews		
Reviews and Compilations		
Succession Planning and Buy/Sell Agreements		
Tax Compliance		
Tax Planning		

EXHIBIT 5-4: IDENTIFY SERVICES USED BY CLIENTS

Services Used By (Client's Name)

Services	Current	Potential
Audit Services		
Audited Retirement or Health or Welfare Plan		
Bankruptcy		
Benefits Consultation		
Bookkeeping and Accounting Services		
Business Consulting		
Business Expansion		
Business Valuations		
Cash Flow Analysis and Budgeting		
Computer Consulting		
Debt Refinancing		
Debt Share Reorganization		
Estate and Retirement Planning		
Financial Planning		
Forecasts and Financing		
Information Brokering		
Internal Control Review		
Inventory		
Litigation Support Services		
Management Advisory Services		
On-line Access for Tax, Accounting and Management, Research Libraries		
Payroll and Sales Tax Reviews		
Reviews and Compilations		
Succession Planning and Buy/Sell Agreements		
Tax Compliance		
Tax Planning		

Don't Be Afraid to Ask

It is unlikely that clients or associates do not want to give you leads or referrals. Usually, the thought never enters their minds. You want to plant a seed by asking for referrals and leads. This assumes, of course, that your work is good and your relationships are positive. It also assumes that in turn you are constantly looking for ways to refer others to your clients and contacts.

Your ability to ask for referrals will be based on several factors: your comfort with your clients and colleagues; your confidence about the benefits of the work you do; your selling skills; and your attitude toward helping people build profitable businesses.

The key may lie with your selling skills. Frequent reviews and evaluation help keep you on target. The "Suggested Reading and Resources for Your Firm Library" section in the back of this book can help get you started.

REVIEW AND EVALUATE PROGRESS

It is important to know how you are doing in order to maintain your level of enthusiasm and interest. Motivation is key in succeeding because it helps maintain your focus. If you have computerized your contact management system, then it can give you an accurate accounting of your progress. If you have a mentor within the firm, have that person give you feedback on your marketing activities and progress. Review your evaluations, goals, and objectives, and your weekly worksheets.

Getting Constructive Feedback

Feedback will let you know what and when you have done well. Getting someone else's input will help you concentrate on needed improvements. It will sharpen your focus. Constructive feedback gives us the opportunity to learn how others might have approached the same situation, the same marketing objectives.

The emphasis should be on continuous improvement, both in your relationship skills and your marketing activities. Feedback and evaluation can take many forms, including the following.

- After a luncheon meeting, make notes about what was talked about, and whether it moved you closer to your goal.
- After a client meeting, ask a colleague who was also in attendance to give you feedback.
- After a formal presentation, ask for an evaluation and make notes for improvement.
- If the presentation of a proposal does not get you the job, analyze why, and how it might be handled differently.

65

- Once you have written an article, get someone from your target readership to review it.
- Ask someone knowledgeable in table manners and dining to evaluate your manners the next time you dine together.
- Gather information on the community organizations where you could use your skills and volunteer effectively.
- Tape your presentations for later evaluation.

Everyone has an idea on how things should be done, but each of us also has a unique style. Some people let ego and pride get in the way of other people's advice and feedback. By being receptive to input from others, you will develop positive habits and effective skills. The important question is the following. Have you been effectively working your plan? Make necessary adjustments, lay out your plan of action for the next period of time, and commit to working it.

■ ■ ■

Keep the following in mind when working your plan.

- This is a continuous process you will pursue throughout your career.
- Start small and work your way up.
- Information about your network must be captured in some fashion.
- Keep track of your progress.
- Look into contact management software.
- Devote at least one lunch a week to networking.
- Be familiar with all the services your firm offers and identify the experts in the firm.
- Look for ways to expand services with existing clients.
- Turn every contact into a marketing opportunity.
- Always look for ways to better serve your clients.
- Review and evaluate progress regularly—seek input from a mentor within the firm.
- Do not be afraid to adjust or change an activity that is not working.
- Do not stop working your plan . . . it will pay off.

ESSENTIAL SKILLS FOR BUILDING QUALITY BUSINESS RELATIONSHIPS

"People are anxious to improve their circumstances, but are unwilling to improve themselves; they therefore remain bound."

— *James Allen, philosopher, from* As A Man Thinketh

"As I grow older I pay less attention to what men say. I just watch what they do."

— *Andrew Carnegie*

It is interesting to note that Andrew Carnegie was personally responsible for developing more corporate leaders than any other man of his time or since. One key trait he looked for was their ability to get along with others.

People do business with people they like and trust. What is it that makes some people likeable and others not? How do we sense a person who is trustworthy and honest? What influences integrity?

Effective relationship skills for success in business have been studied and written about for years. From Peter Drucker to Stephen Covey, from Marilyn Moats Kennedy to Tom Peters, from the University of Michigan to the University of Oregon, people have identified traits common to effective human relations.

There are twelve skills and attributes that are associated with exceptional ability in interpersonal relationships and that make a person an attractive business partner. Some are self-focused, the rest are other-focused, and each is addressed in the sections that follow.

SELF-FOCUSED SKILLS

The first five skills relate to the individual's inner focus—the relationship that everyone has with him or herself. It is widely believed that before one can expect to be effective with others, one must master the self-focused skills of—

1. Having strong character traits.
2. Taking personal responsibility for one's own attitude and actions.
3. Setting and pursuing goals.
4. Practicing self-discipline.
5. Embracing high standards rather than perfectionism.

A detailed discussion of each of these traits follows.

Possesses Strong Character Traits

Strong character traits are based on the fundamental idea that certain principles, such as trust, honesty, and integrity, govern human effectiveness. Trust and honesty are essential to cooperation and long-term personal and interpersonal growth. Integrity pertains to consistency in word, action, and beliefs. A person who exhibits strong traits of character is clear about what they value and believe in. These traits are also clear to others.

Having a clear understanding of your own values and beliefs drives your behaviors and actions and makes daily decision making easier. This consistency is the basis or foundation of integrity. "The Integrity Model," shown as figure 6–1, provides a graphic example. Webster defines integrity as (1) the quality or state of being complete; wholeness; (2) the quality or state of being of sound moral principle; uprightness, honesty, and sincerity.[9] Another view is having everything in sync, working together to get you where you want to go in your particular industry or profession. No matter how you examine integrity, it will follow a specific model.

FIGURE 6-1: THE INTEGRITY MODEL

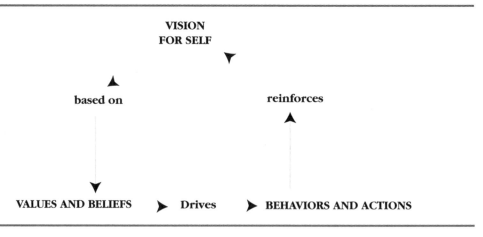

There are three cornerstones for this model: our sense of self (self-esteem), our values and beliefs, and our actions and behaviors. Each is examined in the following sections.

Sense of Self

Each of us has some idea of how we want to think of ourselves. Self-esteem is how one values oneself, and it can also be described as self-worth, the belief and pride in oneself, or one's self-respect. Self-esteem is the measure of one's belief in one's ability to think and cope with life's challenges.

Nathaniel Branden, in his book, *The Psychology of Self-Esteem,* describes it this way: Self-esteem is the key to success or failure. Self-esteem, more than any other single factor, determines how high in life we are likely to rise, emotionally, financially, creatively, spiritually. So in this world, the first love affair that we have to consummate successfully is a love affair with ourselves.[10]

---

[9] *Webster's New World Dictionary of the American Language.* New York: The World Publishing Co., 1966.

[10] Nathaniel Branden. *The Psychology of Self-Esteem.* New York: Bantam Doubleday Publishing Group, 1971.

Values and Beliefs

Your values and beliefs reflect a vital part of who you are. They represent the foundation for your actions. They are not something to have, rather something to be. The vast majority of Americans recognize the following virtues as fundamental indicators of character: respect, honesty, responsibility, fairness, compassion, courage, and perseverance.

The following are some things we know about values.[11]

- Ninety percent of your values were formed by the time you had reached the age of ten.
- The remaining 10 percent of your values were locked in by your twentieth birthday.
- Values are difficult to change. It usually takes a significant emotional event to change your values.
- Values are conditional. A person does not have a defined hierarchy for their values.
- Values influence your behaviors and actions.
- Values influence your attitude about work.

Looking at your values can help you understand how you interact with people at home and work. You are your values. Knowing what is most important to you, and why, can be helpful when making meaningful decisions and for developing effective relationships. It is tough to make decisions about work, recreation, home, and interpersonal relationships without first knowing what is most important to you.

People who are confused and unclear about their values often have difficulty making the bigger decisions in life because they do not know themselves well enough to decide what would be best for them. Values are like maps that guide us.

Actions and Behaviors

This part of integrity addresses what you actually do. It is the observable part of your life. It is what others see or experience of us. From this, they then make judgments about who you are. From your actions and behaviors, others attribute character traits by identifying you as, for instance, honest or dishonest, trustworthy or untrustworthy, straightforward or evasive, sincere or insincere, compassionate or insensitive, hardworking or lazy, and competent or incompetent.

The integrity model shown on page 71 is another way to examine values. Your vision for self (self-esteem) is based on your values and

---

[11] Morris Massey, Ph.D. *What You Are What You Were When*. Morris Massey Associates, Inc., Boulder, Colorado, 1976.

beliefs. The core values and beliefs of any person drive his or her behaviors and actions, which reinforces the sense of self.

If your behaviors are out of sync with your values, your sense of self is influenced. If your self-esteem is low, your work, your outlook on life, your relationships with others, and your integrity are affected.

Let me give you an example that is common today. We are bombarded with information and knowledge about what it takes to lead a healthy life: regular exercise; stress reduction; a good, varied diet; avoidance or reduction of harmful activities such as smoking, drinking, and ingesting known carcinogens.

Many people would tell you that they concur, that health is high on the list of their values. They would add that their behaviors reflect a commitment to this belief.

At the same time, even though life expectancy has improved, we Americans are carrying more extra weight than ever before. We are also more stressed. We struggle with the guilt every time we eat a fatty meal, and take pride in the times that we choose a low-fat alternative instead. We are buying and using—but also storing in our basements and garages—more exercise equipment than ever. We feel compelled to justify our failure to exercise by explaining that our schedules are busy and stressful.

What may this mean? That many of us are actually out of touch with what we value most? That health may not truly hold the value we say it does? That our attempts to live a healthy life are a response to peer pressure—one of the many "shoulds" in our lives?

The point here is that by understanding our values and beliefs, and living a life that reflects those values and reinforces our sense of self, we bring purpose to our lives. Purpose helps us be more consistent in word and deed. We are more likely to "walk our talk."

Consistent behavior and a reputation for integrity can be your greatest assets. Your behaviors and actions give others a glimpse into your character. People with strong character do not compromise their personal value systems, yet they recognize cultural diversity and respect differences among people.

Takes Personal Responsibility for Attitude and Actions

Personal accountability for behaviors, feelings, and outcomes is the focus of this skill. Inner-directed people believe that they themselves largely determine the direction their lives take—a direction determined by the inner characteristics, attitudes, and resources they develop during their lifetime.

The adage, "If you think you can, or you think you can't, you're right," addresses the power of attitude. Positive thinking is seen as possibility thinking. If you do not think you can bring in business, there is a good chance you will not. Not because you are unable to, but because your attitude affects (or infects) your behaviors.

The Hay Group, when identifying outstanding performers, found that attitude, the way outstanding performers think about something, was a critical attribute.[12] The core of an *achievement orientation* is whether or not the person *thinks* about meeting and beating goals and taking calculated risks for measured gains.

Many people feel that their future is largely determined by others, namely, the institutions, organizations, environment, people, situations, and the circumstances in which they happen to find themselves. They tend to rationalize and justify, use cop-outs and excuses, and their talk is negative.

Someone who takes personal responsibility knows that he or she has a choice, and, therefore, consciously chooses attitudes and actions. He or she is proactive and develops the ability to choose responses. Such a person is a product of values and decisions, rather than moods and conditions, and tends to be upbeat, positive, and aware that each action has a consequence. In addition, he or she works to establish positive habits and understands that 90 percent or more of all that we do is dictated by habit. Once a habit is formed, good or bad, one becomes comfortable with it. Once comfortable with it, one then strives to remain consistent, even when habits lead to failure. That makes everyone fairly resistant to change, even beneficial change.

The skill of taking personal responsibility also affects how one models behavior that will be adopted by others. Whether they are parents, spouses, managers, or leaders, people with this skill realize they are role models, and they constantly ask themselves whether they are behaving in a manner they want copied.

Sets and Pursues Goals

Personal effectiveness, the habit of self-management, is an essential skill for anyone in business. It starts with a clear understanding of your desired direction and destination. Where do you want to go? What do you want to accomplish? People who set goals, as outlined in chapter 4, "Developing a Personal Marketing Plan," tend to create things mentally *before* physically. They have a vision, a dream. But it is not enough to dream or have a vision of where you want to go, what you want to accomplish. To be effective, goals must be written down, reviewed, evaluated, and actively pursued.

Setting and pursuing goals leads to better time management. This involves making the most productive use of all your time. When you

---

[12] HayMcBer, The Hay Group, Arlington, VA.

are in the midst of tax season, with working papers and engagements up to your eyeballs, it may be hard to imagine having planned your time. This is not unusual; many of us wait until things reach a crisis stage before tackling them. At the same time, effective time management is necessary as you begin to delegate to others. Effective managers and partners not only manage their time well, but also find it necessary in order to delegate.

A good example of time planning is to plan your week in advance . . . on Friday afternoon or Sunday evening. In addition to planning for your technical work, decide who you want to meet for lunch, when you can fit it in, and schedule the call. Address envelopes to those to whom you want to drop a quick note of thanks or acknowledgment. Schedule time to brainstorm an article you want to write. With planning, your week should be pretty much blocked out with your work and goals in mind.

With a clear focus on goals, your effort and time are spent on activities that will help reach your objectives. It means you spend time on what is most important to you, and that you use your spare time well. As you reach your goals, you start to go through the same process all over again. It is a lifelong pattern.

Practices Self-Discipline

This skill is your ability to stay focused. The need to concentrate is grounded in the consideration that there are always more important contributions to be made than there is time in which to make them. There is a richness of important tasks. There will always be a shortage of time to do them all.

Self-discipline is integral to being consistent in behavior and actions based on your values. To be true to yourself and to stay on track requires self-control. It can be easy to be swayed by the situation, society, peer pressure, or a lack of focus.

That does not mean pursuing goals at the expense of spontaneity and flexibility. Rather, it allows you to be flexible, responsive, and able to change direction quickly. It is reflected in your ability to be *mentally* present where you are *physically* present. Worriers have not mastered this skill. They spend mental time in the future—worrying, instead of focusing on the task, event, or emotion at hand. They spend time worrying about what they *could* or *should* be doing instead of focusing on what they *are* doing.

Self-control means being in control of your emotions and feelings as well. We have all heard that patience is a virtue, but some of us find it hard to practice. We must learn to routinely separate our feelings about people's actions from our feelings about the people themselves.

Embraces High Standards Versus Perfectionism

High standards give us the opportunity to perform at our best. Perfection, on the other hand, involves trying to attain the impossible—striving for unattainable results, setting oneself up for continuing disappointment. A person who holds to high standards is guided by these standards, in order to reach their full potential. This also involves having a good self-assessment of strengths and weaknesses—knowing what you are indeed capable of doing well.

A person who embraces high standards continually seeks feedback. Without it, they do not believe that they have a true perspective of how they are doing. Feedback serves as checks on the path to success. A person with high standards is not afraid to hear the truth and seek out those who tell it. Often, a person who sets unrealistic standards for themselves also does so for others.

OTHER-FOCUSED SKILLS

The seven other-focused skills pertain to the individual's ability to relate to others. These strong interpersonal skills affect communication, productivity, cooperation, and leadership, and entail—

1. Having a sense of fairness.
2. Being an effective communicator.
3. Appreciating and valuing others.
4. Exhibiting social skills and poise.
5. Believing in potential and growth.
6. Seeing relationships as interdependent rather than dependent.
7. Stimulating action.

Has a Sense of Fairness

Here the concept of equity and justice prevails. This skill is based on consistency in applying rules and policies, keeping human dignity in mind. The person with a developed sense of fairness looks to themselves before blaming others. It is the philosophy that "The buck stops here." Often, people look to others to place blame.

At home, if you want to use the scissors or any other tool and can't find them, do you ask yourself, "Who didn't put the scissors back?" or "Where did I last use those scissors?" The way you answer this gives a clue as to how you react in the workplace as well. Applying this in the workplace tends to focus on results, which is empowering. Make a point of doing the right things rather than doing things right. This means you do not play favorites. Regardless of your personal feelings, you want to be seen and acknowledged as fair and evenhanded.

Is an Effective Communicator

Communication skills rank second only to job knowledge as important factors in a businessperson's success. Everything we do depends on the successful transfer of meaning from one person or group to another. Interpersonal communication skills reflect the ability to continuously build credibility and believability into everything we communicate. Although we were taught reading and writing before leaving school, most of us were not given instruction on listening and speaking. The average businessperson spends as much as 85 percent of the day communicating in some form—with less than 30-percent efficiency. This skill is where your ability to influence, persuade, and direct shines.

Listening Skills

Listening and hearing are two different things. Most people rate themselves as good listeners. However, we spend most of our time listening, not with the intent of understanding, but rather with the intent of replying—preparing to speak. Our goal is to *be understood*. The goal of effective listening is *to understand*—to ultimately seek mutual understanding.

Writing Skills

A common complaint heard in corporate America is that business professionals no longer know how to write properly. A rich vocabulary and a command of English grammar dictate how far you will go in your career. Your choice of words in varying situations reflects your education and effectiveness in communicating.

Speaking Skills

Whether you are speaking before a large group or to one other person, you communicate through your words, how you sound, and what you look like when you are speaking. Being able to express your ideas and thoughts effectively means being in control of both your verbal and nonverbal behaviors.

The ability to make an effective presentation may require you to be persuasive or informational, depending on the outcome you are seeking. Solid speaking skills enable you to effectively make your point whether at a meeting, interview, client conference, or at a performance review, lunch break, or press conference.

Appreciates and Values Others

This attribute focuses on an appreciation for and an understanding of the values of others. It means embracing a sensitivity for other cultures, beliefs, and traditions. You value others' experience, ideas, ways of analyzing problems, and the creative solutions they bring to the workplace. You affirm, enjoy, and value the uniquenesses of every individual.

Because of this, it is important for you to bring differing perspectives together in the spirit of mutual respect—teamwork and cooperation. Empathy is one of your strong points—your ability to get inside another person's frame of reference.

Exhibits Social Skills and Poise

Because the United States is a heterogeneous society with many regional, racial, and cultural differences, we learn to adjust—to use our social skills so we do not inadvertently offend others or embarrass ourselves. Diplomacy is knowing how to act in someone else's ballpark, playing by their rules, rather than imposing our own.

Being poised allows us to feel comfortable doing so, whether in a formal setting or an informal one. Self-assurance is a reflection of our self-confidence. The tact and diplomacy that are part of gracious social skills allow us to put others at ease, making them feel valued and important, and build rapport.

LEADERSHIP-FOCUSED SKILLS

Leadership is presented separately because it is important to distinguish these skills as a reminder of leadership responsibility.

Believes in Potential and Growth

Not only must you believe in your own potential, putting it into practice by improving skills and gaining new talents, but you must encourage it in others. Expecting the best of the people around you will be rewarded with great things. To do this, you understand that the way you treat others will influence their performance and career progress. You have the ability to communicate expectations positively, knowing most people live up to what is expected of them. And you revel in the accomplishments of others.

You believe growth comes from going beyond our limits, taking risks, and making mistakes. Therefore, you encourage others to make decisions, take risks, and grow. You recognize the importance of positive reinforcement and praise and look for ways to use these incentives with others.

Sees Relationships As Interdependent Rather Than Independent

This skill focuses on our ability to cooperate. It is based on a mentality of *abundance* and *prosperity*, rather than *scarcity*, and the assumption that there are solutions and options to help people reach mutually satisfying solutions.

Collaborative, win/win thinking is essential to seeing relationships as interdependent. Independence can result in win/no win outcomes, something done at the expense of others. Interdependence strives for a win/win or at least a win/win or no deal option. Seeking mutual benefit is one of the strengths of this skill—the ability to seek synergistic solutions, those that are agreeable to both parties.

A belief that the whole is greater than the sum of its parts leads to strong teamwork. Encouraging people to make work-related choices fosters job ownership and a sense of responsibility for productivity and quality. Creative cooperation helps in building rich, enduring, highly productive relationships with other people.

Stimulates Action

Moving others to action, getting employees to buy into a vision or goal, getting people to get the right things done, or persuading clients to buy more services, all require influence. This skill enables one to have an impact on others, to influence or persuade them to action.

Several factors come into play here. A person must be able to see the bigger picture, break it down, and communicate it in terms of the overall vision. One must be able to coach and draw on the expertise and skills of others in moving toward that vision or goal. It includes the ability to understand others' motivation in order to appeal to their interests and needs. It includes respect—respecting others and being respected oneself.

Since these attributes or skills are common to those who are effective at building quality relationships, it would be a good idea to see how you would rate yourself in each of the categories as shown in exhibit 6-1. Look at each skill, review the descriptions above, and rate yourself on a scale of 1 to 5, using 1 to mean "Say, what?" while 5 means "Have this one down pat."

EXHIBIT 6-1: EVALUATION TOOL—ESSENTIAL SKILLS FOR BUILDING QUALITY RELATIONSHIPS

	Rating: 1-5	Work on This One Now
1. Strong character ethics		
2. Personal responsibility and accountability		
3. Sets goals		
4. Self-discipline		
5. High standards versus perfectionism		
6. Sense of fairness		
7. Effective communication skills ■ Listening skills ■ Writing skills ■ Speaking skills		
8. Values others		
9. Social skills and poise		
10. Believes in potential and growth		
11. Sees relationships as interdependent		
12. Stimulates action		

Which of these skills did you rate the lowest?

Which of these skills did you rate the highest?

Which ones do you feel need the most work today, for where you are in your career? (These may not be the ones rated lowest.)

If you were to have a mentor or colleague rate you, how might his or her ratings be different from yours?

By evaluating your interpersonal relationship skills, you will have a better understanding of what it takes to build and nurture strong business relations with clients, colleagues, and associates. It will, hopefully, get you thinking about the importance of making yourself likeable and trustworthy, and being accountable for how others perceive you.

■ ■ ■

Keep the following in mind when when building interpersonal skills.

■ Mastery of self is a prerequisite to being effective with others.

■ By clarifying values, decision making becomes easier.

■ People want to be fairly treated.

■ Setting goals gives you direction.

■ Self-discipline helps accomplish what you want to achieve.

■ High self-esteem means you value and believe in yourself.

■ Your self-esteem is affected by your actions and behaviors.

■ People observe what you do and make judgments about your character.

■ Do as you say you will do.

■ Do not expect yourself or others to be perfect—it is unrealistic.

■ Your ability to listen well is key to client satisfaction.

■ Reread Strunk & White's *The Elements of Style* to refresh your ability to express yourself on paper.

■ Practice tact and diplomacy.

■ Learn to look for each person's uniqueness.

■ Set a good example for those who observe you.

MANAGING
THE MINGLING

*"Eighty percent of success
is showing up."*

—Woody Allen, filmmaker and actor

As you might guess, almost no one enjoys walking into a room full of strangers; most people dread it more than engaging one stranger in small talk. Yet, in order to expand business contacts, everyone needs to attend events, meetings, and gatherings of strangers. Whether it is one's first state society meeting, or a monthly meeting of an association of general contractors, the fears and feelings can be the same.

Even the most gregarious person has moments of shyness, but how that shyness is expressed varies. Some people become wall-flowers; others affect arrogance. Still others attach—and confine—themselves to people they already know. The first step toward overcoming these and other counterproductive reactions is to acknowledge that they conceal underlying feelings of awkwardness and discomfort in the presence of strangers.

Since mingling is an integral part of meeting people, anyone, with a little planning, can learn to enjoy the process and make it work for them. Not only is it important to show up, as Woody Allen points out, but it is also important to be there mentally. People who get ahead in business create connections deliberately and professionally.

TAKE TIME TO PREPARE

As Susan RoAne points out in her book, *How to Work a Room*, a person must take time to plan his or her presence.[13] Both your effectiveness and enjoyment will be directly related to the amount of time and the thought you give to the function itself. If there is no purpose, why bother going? Take time to ask yourself the following questions.

- Why am I going?
- Who will be there?
- What is the purpose of the event?
- What do I want to gain by being there?
- Am I presentable?
- Am I in the right frame of mind?

It is important to understand the purpose or benefit of attending a function, whether it is a board meeting, association meeting, cocktail party, or Chamber of Commerce event. The benefits will vary depending on the type of function. Even if you sit in your car for five minutes reflecting on the questions above before entering the event, you will benefit. Let's examine the value of each question.

---

[13] Susan RoAne. *How to Work a Room.* New York: Shapolsky Publishers, Inc., 1988.

WHY AM I GOING?

This is an important question to ask of every event or meeting you commit to. It focuses on the benefits. There are many reasons why it may be important to be there, including the following.

- It is expected of you as part of your job.
- Your competition will be there.
- Your clients and important referral sources will be there.
- You want to show support for the event, person, or organization.
- You want to be seen within your industry or profession.
- You want to be seen within your client's industry.
- You are a role model for others within the firm and you want to underline the importance of networking to make connections.
- It supports an interest of yours.

Professionally, you benefit from showing up at events and meeting people for a wide range of reasons. Attending events—

- Expands your network of contacts and resources.
- Helps build your self-confidence and social skills.
- Enhances your credibility and visibility with others in the profession, industry, or with clients.
- Builds and nurtures your existing relationships.
- Enhances your career opportunities and earning power.
- Increases your knowledge base and expands your interests.
- Creates fun times.

Once you identify the benefits and truly believe in them, mingling becomes easier, more enjoyable, and brings positive results. Adopt a positive attitude. Get in the right frame of mind. Take on the attitude of an explorer who is looking for people, ideas, and resources that can help add value to your work-related goals. The flip side of this role is to figure out what you have to offer others. Remember, it is a two-way street.

WHAT I WANT AND WHAT I HAVE TO OFFER

Having a goal or two in mind before you head into a room full of people is an effective way to realize benefits. What you want to know and learn, the people you want to meet, the places you want to go, the connections you want to make—all are examples of the kinds of things everyone wants. Translating these into goals for a meeting or event helps add purpose and supports the benefits of being there. These goals do not need to be only professional; they can also be personal.

Chart 7-1 is an example of some of the professional and personal goals you might have identified beforehand. The professional goals should tie into your marketing plan from chapter 4, "Developing a Personal Marketing Plan." The personal goals usually reflect what's going on in your life outside of the workplace—hobbies, interests, vacations, day-to-day activities. Both will assist you with small talk and conversation.

CHART 7-1: PROFESSIONAL AND PERSONAL GOALS

Professional Goals	*Personal Goals*
Meet someone in the hospitality industry	Find a good orthodontist (you need one)
Meet a client's banker	Tips on traveling to Bali (you're going there)
Contact management software user	Tips on growing tomatoes (a new interest)
Create a Web site on Internet	Night spots for western dancing (a new interest)
Get a part-time administrative person	Authentic Mexican restaurant (favorite ethnic food)
Look for new career opportunities	House sitter for pets (need one for vacation trip)
Find someone to edit articles	Best bicycle for all-around use (a new interest)

By approaching the event and the subsequent small talk as a way to seek out what you want, you will expand your capacity to enjoy conversations, satisfying contacts, interesting subjects, and exchange of ideas and information.

The other half of the equation concerns what you have to offer others. What kinds of experiences have you had? Where have you traveled? What are your hobbies? Most people have a hard time seeing themselves as interesting in the first place. But stop and take a harder look at your interests, skills, contacts, and expertise. You will find you have a lot to offer others. Chart 7-2 gives an example.

CHART 7-2: WHAT I CAN OFFER

What I Can Offer Professionally	What I Can Offer Personally
Starting own business	Great wines (you are a gourmand)
Internet experience	Golf schools in the West (tried several)
Networking computers	Real estate agent specializing in condos (friend)
Desktop publishing	Terrific B&B in Montana (first-hand experience)
Financial planning	Source for Wheaton Terriers (own two)
Strong contacts in construction industry	Remodeling pitfalls (been there, done that)
Succession planning	Exercises to strengthen back (my success)

You may not actually take the time to write all this down each time you attend a meeting or function. However, if you give it some thought beforehand, the process of meeting others, exploring topics, and exchanging information becomes more interesting and fun.

ESTABLISH AN AGENDA

Now that you have an idea of what you want and what you can offer, establish some goals or an agenda specific for the event or meeting. You do not need to have a long list, but rather just two or three goals. Maybe one is business related, and the others personal. As we discussed in chapter 4, goals keep us focused.

If you are attending a state society meeting, perhaps you want to meet someone on the board to find out more about the time and commitment it takes. Or you want to get involved with a political action committee, so meeting someone who is on that committee would be beneficial. Maybe you need to find a CPA who specializes in Native American corporations.

If you sit on the board of a nonprofit and are attending a board meeting, a goal might be to find another board member who could introduce you to a particular person—a business owner you are interested in pursuing as a client, or a lawyer who would be a great resource to your firm.

If you are at a trade show or convention, you may want to meet a CPA from a particular part of the country in which one of your clients has business. Or you may want to meet a CPA involved in the industry in which you specialize. These people can become valuable resources.

A personal goal, if you are in an unfamiliar city, might be to find a good restaurant or museum, an interesting place to jog, or a nightspot that plays jazz. Perhaps you are looking for a reliable electrician or plumber. Ask. Put it out. Bring it up in the conversation.

People feel good when they can assist someone else. It does not cost anything to recommend a good plumber or orthodontist. These goals do not put others on the spot to hire you or buy your services. They are safe subjects of interest for both parties. Even if I cannot recommend a good electrician, I may know someone who has recently remodeled. This gives me the opportunity to help you out.

For the more advanced networker, one who is skilled at business development, it is important to qualify your prospect. At events and meetings, you do not have a lot of time to spend with each individual you meet. Therefore, if you want to maximize your time, you also must learn to gauge the quality of a particular contact.

Thomas Stanley, a Georgia State professor, reports in his book, *Marketing to the Affluent*, that one of the most common traits of the 2,000 millionaires he studied was the size of their Rolodex®.[14] He also found they had an "uncanny ability to distinguish quality contacts." Not only do they collect business cards, but they can identify the people who are able and willing to help them, the people with whom they can share support, information, and business opportunities.

Working the room effectively for the experienced means they have a short list of qualifying questions to see if it is worth spending more time with this person. While your prospect is talking, ask yourself the following questions. What does he or she need (and do I sell it)? What is his or her motivation (why would he or she want me)? What is his or her budget (can he or she afford me)?

The key to qualifying is to let the other person do the talking. If you can come up with satisfactory answers to the preceding questions, it is worth spending time with this person.

Developing good conversational skills that engage others is explored in greater detail in the next chapter.

---

[14] Thomas Stanley. *Marketing to the Affluent*. Homewood, IL: Dow Jones, 1988.

PLAN YOUR SELF-INTRODUCTION

One thing we can be sure of is that people want to know who you are, what you do, and why you are there. This is a natural process that takes place when we meet new people. An effective self-introduction creates interest and gives others a basis for further conversation.

Typically, what we hear is the following.

> "Hello, my name is Dana Jarvis. I'm a CPA working for Bradson & Associates."

It might be more engaging to say this:

> "Hello, I'm Dana Jarvis, a CPA. This is my first meeting and I'm looking forward to finding out more about the association."

The difference has to do with the additional information. This is often referred to as a *tag line*. A tag line gives more information than just the name. It helps others identify you with something, someplace, or someone. The following are examples.

■ *Identify with an event or function.* The following tag line explains the relationship based on a *past* connection.

> "Hi, I'm Jeff Smith. We worked on the Boys and Girls Club fundraising auction together last year."

■ *Identify with a place.* This example tells the other person that you are there because of a *location* connection.

> "Hello, my name is Carol and I work in the same building."

■ *Identify with a person.* This example clarifies the relationship and reinforces the *personal* connection.

> "Hi, my name is Richard Shank and I work with Bill Smith."

■ *Identify with one of your goals.* This example tells the other person how they might help you with an interest or information connection.

> "Hi, I'm Barbara Schmidt and I'm here to learn more about Web sites."

If you simply add a tag line that gives the name of your company, it often does not work as well. You do not want to put people on the spot or make them feel stupid for not knowing what the company is or does. A better way of stating your name and company might sound like the following.

> "Hello, my name is Dana Jarvis. My company helps businesses set up foreign corporations. I'm a CPA with Bradson & Associates."

Job-related tag lines that work best are often benefit-oriented or create interest. Effective tag lines that work for CPAs (in order to engage others) are the following.

■ I bring peace of mind to small business owners.

■ I help make sense of numbers.

■ I help businesses grow profitably.

■ I take the confusion out of the tax laws.

■ My work involves raising capital for business expansions.

■ I help put business owners in touch with money sources.

You want to focus on the problems you can solve, the benefits to your clients, and your achievements, not your job description. Tag lines such as these open the lines of communication. You give the others a point of reference from which they can launch into questions or make comments. Examples are the following.

"Tell me more about that."

"What is your educational background?"

"Will you give me an example?"

These same tag lines can be used successfully when you are asked that common cliché question, "What do you do?"

The key to self-introductions, even though they are not more than ten to fifteen seconds in length, is to give people information that they can use to extend the conversation and build rapport.

PLAN FOR SMALL TALK

Engaging others in interesting conversation seldom happens without some forethought. You want to prepare some interesting tidbits. Basically, you will want to tell others about yourself, discover something about others, and find common ground. Read the paper, do your homework on the event and the people involved, tap into your goals, and have in mind anecdotes from past experiences. The following section describes techniques that will help you organize your thoughts as they relate to the particular meeting or event you are attending.

Inner-Oriented Topics

Inner-oriented topics generally fall into two categories: what I'm thinking and what I want or need (going back to your goals for the event). Let's look at each to see how we can use them to initiate conversation.

What I'm Thinking

The following are examples of thoughts you might use as the point of departure for remarks about what you are thinking.

■ Make a comment about yourself:

"This is my first meeting and I'm looking forward to meeting the others on the board."

■ Make a comment about what you're thinking:

"I'm surprised by how many people turned out for this. How many usually attend?"

■ Make a statement about yourself or your experience.

"I've always found that I pick up good business pointers at these Chamber roundtables. What has been your experience?"

■ Share a story or personal anecdote.

"Traveling during the holidays was quite an experience for us. I learned a few things I plan to keep in mind for that next holiday trip."

What I need or want

The following are examples of what you want or need that might be the basis for small talk.

■ Make a statement about a specific area of information you're after.

"I've just recently moved into town and am looking for a dentist close to work or my apartment. Do you know of any in the Ballard or Capital Hill areas?"

■ Ask a question about one of your goals.

"I've been wanting to meet more of the major players in the hospitality industry. You seem to know most everyone here. Who would you suggest? Would you introduce me?"

Outward-Oriented Topics

Outward-oriented topics focus on what you observe, see, and what others experience or think. You want to think in terms of what you see in the room or office, on desks, what people are wearing, environmental observations (such as the weather, the location itself, or the political climate), themes, the people attending, and so on. Bring up trends, current affairs, and the purpose of the occasion to give others the opportunity to comment on these topics and help establish a common ground.

What you see or observe

The following are examples of topics that are drawn from what you or others observe and experience.

■ Make a comment or statement.

"That's a beautiful pin (or unusual trophy, interesting painting). What's the story behind it?"

■ Share your observation.

"There seems to be a good turnout for this meeting. Is it the topic and speaker?"

■ Ask an open-ended question.

"Why have you decided to serve on the Children's Hospital Board?"

What You Would Like Others to Comment On

■ Share an anecdote.

"My pager activated during the church service last weekend. It seems we just can't get away from work-related issues anymore. How do you cope with the demand for your time?"

■ Ask a question.

"How does your company use benchmarking to improve the quality of services you offer?"

■ Make a comment.

"Boy, can you believe the Mariners! Though I'm not an avid baseball fan, I found myself glued to the TV during the pennant series. It's always fun to watch the best teams playing their best games. Did you follow the playoffs?"

■ Expand on trite questions such as, "What's new?"

"I'm getting our boat cleaned up and ready for our summer activities."

"Now that the weather is improving, I'm back out at the driving range to improve my golf game."

"We just implemented a new contact management system, and I'm in the middle of the learning curve."

The value and advantages of doing some homework on the occasion and the people *before* you get to the meeting or event cannot be overemphasized. I once heard a radio interview of Malcolm Forbes, Jr., in which the interviewer asked him about his father's yacht, *The Highlander*. Malcolm Forbes, Sr., frequently did business entertaining on the yacht and his children were invited aboard to entertain the guests with their music. In preparation for the event, Mr. Forbes had each child learn the names of all the guests, who they worked for, and their connection to Forbes and his personal and business interests. This armed the children with information that would not only prove useful in conversation with the guests while aboard, but also was a valuable lesson about people, contacts, power, and influence.

BUSINESS CARD PROTOCOL

The business card is one of the oldest forms of marketing. It is a physical reminder of who you are, what you do, and how you can be reached. It is important and appropriate to have your cards handy, and to give them out.

Before you leave your office for a meeting, always check to see that you have several clean cards with you. If you are off to a trade show or large meeting, make sure you take plenty of business cards along. You might want to keep extras in your car and your briefcase just in case you find yourself without cards in your purse or wallet.

At meetings and functions, it is not appropriate to keep a wad of cards in your hand and give one to every person you see. A common mistake is giving out cards freely and giving them too soon. Another mistake is not having business cards on hand to leave with a person. Just because you gave someone your business card does not mean you have made a business connection. Think about how many times you have fished out a business card from your pocket or purse and wondered who this person was.

The best time to exchange business cards is when some connection is made between two people—some reason to exchange names and telephone numbers. Through your conversational skills, you try to uncover common ground. Generally, this has to do with the goals each of you have for this event or meeting. If you see yourself as an explorer, you might be asking yourself the following questions. Why is this person here? What do they need? How might I help? Can they provide me with assistance on my goals?

One of the best reasons to exchange cards is to extend the relationship beyond the event at which you met. If you ask for someone else's card, note the following on the card as soon as possible (but not in his or her presence):

■ The date and location or event on it

■ Rank of the contact for quality as a lead or resource (A for hot, C for okay)

■ Anything you have promised

■ Any reminders of the person and his or her interests

By writing the date on all cards you receive, you will always be able to identify which of your colleagues' cards are the most current and when you met the person. The likelihood of timely follow-up on any promises is much higher if you have made notes on the card. The information can also be entered into your contact management database.

When do you give your card to someone else? When they have asked for it or offered to provide you with information or a contact. If they mention that they know someone who could help you with your desktop publishing, you might reply, " Would you mind if I called you for her name? Let me give you my card, as well, to pass along to her."

Or perhaps you can provide some assistance to the other person. You might give them your card and say, "I know a Japanese art dealer who might be a good resource for your customer. Call this week and I will give you her name and phone number."

If you are wearing a suit or jacket with pockets, one method that works for many people is to keep your own business cards in the right-hand pocket, and any cards you receive in the left-hand pocket. Place your cards in a well-placed card case, or in a section of your purse or wallet that is accessible without fumbling.

Do not forget the following.

■ Your business cards are an extension of the image you want to project. They should be well designed, easy to read, and clean.

■ If you are between jobs, the same holds true for your card. Have one printed for networking purposes.

■ Some cultures revere the business card exchange. Maintain a keen sense of observation. Most Asians, especially the Japanese, consider it disrespectful to write on a business card. When a Japanese businessperson is presenting a business card, he or she presents the card with both hands. The printing faces the person receiving the card.

LOOKING THE PART

Your image, the way you are at all moments in time, is a form of communication. You will want to look like the consummate professional you are. Your appearance reflects your pride in yourself and your profession. Creating a positive impression starts with how we look in the eyes of others. This is covered extensively in chapter 10, "Meeting and Greeting People," but merits a few reminders here.

When you go to meetings, do you look like you want to be there? You want to look interested, vital, and prepared. It is absolutely amazing how many people come to a planning session, educational meeting, or board meeting without a pen, pencil, or paper. What kind of message does that send?

What does your posture indicate? Slouching, sloppy posture can send the message that you are uninterested, could care less, and wish you were somewhere else. Posture, the way you sit, stand, walk, and move, is a signal to others about your confidence, status, and power. Use it effectively.

Looking the part also means paying attention to grooming. Many of the meetings and events we attend are at the end of the day. Check your clothes for wrinkles, runs, dandruff, lint, loose hems, scuffs, spills, and spots. Check your makeup, hair, and nails to make sure they are still well-groomed.

Making eye contact and offering a smile is one of the most important gestures a person can exhibit to assist the rapport-building process. Think back to an event you have attended. It is generally the people who make eye contact and smile that we tend to warm up to first. It helps dissolve some of the shyness. It helps make you appear more approachable.

HOW AND WHEN TO FOLLOW UP

Meeting people at functions and events is only of value if that relationship is extended beyond the event itself. And it gives you the opportunity to showcase your reliability and integrity. If you promised something, deliver!

How many times have you heard people say they will call to get together for lunch? And they never call. If you have no intention of going to lunch with someone, or you are too busy, then do not commit to the call or the lunch. Saying you will do something and not following through sends a negative message and kills credibility.

To effectively follow up and keep in touch, develop the habit of taking care of the commitment the moment you get back to your office. Schedule it on your daily calendar. Make notes on the business card, enter it into your electronic Rolodex®, and follow through.

It may be as simple as writing a brief note to the person saying how much you enjoyed meeting them. While we were golfing, my husband and I were teamed up with a prominent Seattle lawyer and his wife. Dale received the following note a few weeks later.

Dear Dale:

Just a note to let you know how much LaRue and I enjoyed golfing with you in Port Ludlow. My schedule since returning has been too hectic to acknowledge the nice afternoon we had with you.

I have saved your card, and hope to catch you for lunch in the not-too-distant future.

Very truly yours,...

That contact and follow-up led to a luncheon and eventually to business beneficial to both Dale's CPA firm and the lawyer's firm. The note is three sentences long and could not have taken even five minutes to write.

Sometimes we promise a contact's name, an article on a topic of interest, or to set up a lunch or meeting. If you can pick up the phone to follow through with your commitment, do so. However, the written word has more impact. If you are not already in the habit of writing notes of thanks or acknowledgment, it is a powerful habit to get into. Tom Peters, in his latest book, *The Power of WOW!*, states the habit of writing notes can be one of the most profitable habits you will ever develop.[15]

Pick up on other people's interests and note the topics of conversation. You might follow up by sending someone an article relating to the topic. It might be on sailing the Greek Isles or trends in the commercial real estate business. You would accompany this unsolicited clipping with a note that might say, "I couldn't help but think of you when I saw this article. I thought you might enjoy reading it."

Any time you take the time to follow up with a telephone call or note, you enhance the opportunity to develop a mutually beneficial relationship. Do not pass up the opportunity. It is an easy way to distinguish yourself from others, because so few people actually do what they say they will do.

[15] Tom Peters. *The Pursuit of WOW!* New York: Vintage Books, 1994.

■ ■ ■

Keep the following in mind when networking and mingling.

- Do plan networking as a business strategy.
- Do seek out people who can add value to your organization.
- Do not use networking events to close a deal.
- Do take time to set some goals for the event.
- Do be willing to share and receive information.
- Do not hand out business brochures at these events.
- Do not engage people in lengthy conversations and discussions.
- Do take time to plan and practice an engaging self-introduction.
- Do present yourself and your firm professionally.
- Do not sit with the people you work with.
- Do remember you are there for the business, not the food.
- Do not ask advice of people who normally get paid for it.
- Do follow up with any promises within three to five days.

FROM SMALL TALK TO ENGAGING CONVERSATION

"A good conversationalist is not one who remembers what was said, but says what someone wants to remember."

—John Mason Brown

"Good communication is as stimulating as black coffee, and just as hard to sleep after."

—Anne Morrow Lindbergh, author

People who study successful people have noted that a person's command of the English language and vocabulary, and his or her ability to engage others in meaningful conversation have a direct effect on advancement. The way one communicates with others is almost as important as the content of the message. Being a good conversationalist is an attractive quality that enhances the ability to influence, persuade, educate, amuse, and motivate others.

Moreover, people like being around good conversationalists and tend to listen to them.

Conversational skills enhance your everyday activities and life's successes, whether by building your career or business, or simply by adding to the enjoyment of conversing with others. You can develop these skills with the following basic requirements:

- A sincere interest in others
- A sincere desire to please and connect with others
- The ability to ask questions
- Active listening skills
- A keen sense of observation

SMALL TALK IS IMPORTANT

When I ask my audiences what it is about small talk that annoys them, most respond that they think small talk is unimportant, inconsequential, and a waste of time. In fact, small talk helps build rapport, bridges conversational topics, and helps put others at ease.

Think about the time you were standing next to someone at an industry meeting and could think of nothing to say. Or when you were tongue-tied at a company dinner, and so was your dinner partner. Or the time everyone sat in awkward silence while waiting for a board or client meeting to start. Or when you were in a car with your superior and the silence was deafening. These are the times when you want to practice your small talk.

People who are adept at small talk are appreciated—and rewarded—all the more because so many others have trouble with it. If you observe the partners who bring in the most business, you are observing a CPA who is skilled at small talk. So what does it take to develop the skill?

DEVELOPING CONVERSATIONAL SKILLS

Now that you understand the benefits of good conversational skills, you are probably more willing to put in the time and effort to develop them. Actually, since we spend so much time talking anyway, how can it hurt to practice effective communication?

The following are suggestions for how you can develop your ability to converse easily.

1. *Read extensively, both in and out of your field.* By reading (and listening to audiotapes), you will be better informed and be able to converse on a wide variety of subjects. This will help you participate, even minimally, in conversations on politics, community activities, the arts, sports, geography, major world news, various industries, and business trends. In contrast, if the only subject you know well is your business, your conversation will be boring.

2. *Develop your curiosity about what others do for a living, what affects their industries, and new directions they might take.* This is especially important for business development. Through conversation, you can uncover your clients' needs and concerns. This gives you the opportunity to better serve them because you understand them better. Besides, people will be flattered by your interest in what interests them.

3. *Do your homework beforehand.* If you take a few minutes to learn about the event, function, or occasion; the people attending; and any other pertinent information, you will be armed with enough solid information for small talk, including conversational tidbits and good questions. It will also help you plan your goals for the event as well.

4. *Develop your ability to ask open-ended questions.* Questions that cannot be answered with just yes or no tend to encourage lengthier conversations that focus on the interests of others. For example, if you ask someone whether he or she has taken a vacation this year, the answer can be a monosyllable. However, if you ask what kind of vacation someone is planning, you are inviting him or her to describe a trip already taken or one being planned. Open-ended questions cannot guarantee that you will get a detailed answer—someone could answer, "I'm not going anywhere" —but these questions increase the likelihood that you will be able to get a conversation started.

   Your ability to ask open-ended questions can also be effective when meeting with clients. If you ask a client whether he or she has any questions or concerns, the answer could be, "No." If instead you ask, for example, "Which industry trends do you think will have the biggest impact on your business?" you may prompt your client to divulge some very real concerns.

5. *Be a good listener and refrain from interrupting.* Most people rate themselves as good listeners. Yet, observation and tests disclose that most people listen with less than 50-percent effectiveness. Good listening skills mean seeking mutual understanding. Remember the saying, "If you want to be listened to, you should put in more time listening."

6. *Develop your ability to use stories, anecdotes, and humor.* Many silences can be broken with a great story or anecdote. They also help bridge conversational topics. Stories are all around you . . . in the news, in books, at work, on the freeway, in the supermarket, and from your own experience as well. An inconsequential event can be turned into a great anecdote. Learn by listening to good conversationalists. Notice how they bring up a topic or story, tell what it is about, and deliver the story.

Humor allows you to laugh with others. It also allows you to laugh at yourself without self-consciousness. Be sensitive, however; joke telling is not always humorous. Remember to be appropriate and avoid offending others. Never embarrass anyone else. Never make someone else the butt of the joke.

7. *Know how to include others in the conversation.* Some people are shy about joining a conversation. Directing specific questions to a person who has not said a word gives him or her a chance to shine as well.

It has been said that a good conversationalist can take the boring and mundane and make it interesting and exciting. However you look at it, the art of conversation and small talk is worth cultivating.

T.A.L.K.—MAKING IT WORK EVERY TIME

You can ease the way for yourself in developing your conversation skills by taking the right approach to your attendance at events. Do some research ahead of time on the occasion and the people who will be there. Keep in mind the following tips, along with your own personal and professional goals.

T = Take the Initiative

Do not wait for others to approach you. Make the first move yourself. Smile, make eye contact, and approach an individual or a small group. Wait for a pause and then introduce yourself. You might say something like the following.

"May I join you? My name is Steve Bassett and this is my first meeting."

"May I join you? I'm Jim Kinnear and couldn't help but overhear your discussion on funding sports stadiums. Very interesting topic these days!"

"Hello, my name is Janice Barber. Have you heard tonight's speaker before?"

A = Attitude . . . Adopt the Attitude of an Explorer

Somewhere in that room, at that meeting, in the convention hall, is someone who can help you meet your goals, and as well as someone you can help. By keeping your goals in mind, your actions are attuned to your purpose. There is more enjoyment in working the room. You see the other guests as interesting people with agendas and goals that need to be met, interests that can be shared. You see the others as resources. You see yourself as a resource to them.

L = Listen and Look (Observe)

Active listening leads to high-quality questions. If you are truly listening to a person, then ideas for further questions become more apparent. Many people give us hints about what interests them in their self-introductions, or comments they make.

"What attracted you to skydiving?"

"Has the equipment changed much over the years?"

"How have environmental concerns affected the fish-processing business?"

"Who is your primary market for surimi?"

"How has your market changed or developed within the last five to ten years?"

Developing your sense of observation is a great way to launch into small talk. Look at the artwork, the location itself, the view, the people in attendance, and what they wear.

"Have you noticed the keen interest in glass art recently?"

"That's an interesting pin. What is the significance of the beads?"

"I never tire of looking at the water. Are you interested in boating?"

K = Keep the Ball Going

When someone throws a topic at you, do not kill the conversational opportunity. If someone asks if you are interested in boating, and you are not, do not just say "No!" You might say, "No, it's never been one of my interests because I've spent a lot of time in the mountains. I enjoy hiking and camping." Or, "No, growing up on a farm in Kansas didn't offer many boating opportunities. What kind of boating do you enjoy?"

If someone asks if you have been with Olsen & Bender long, don't just say, "No, just two years," and drop it. Continue by adding, "I came from private industry before joining this public accounting firm. It gave me some excellent insight into running businesses profitably."

MOVING FROM SMALL TALK TO MORE MEANINGFUL CONVERSATION

In chapter 7, "Managing the Mingling," we discussed several ways to start a conversation. You can focus on what you are thinking and make an observation, comment, or statement. Or you can focus on what you see and observe and ask questions, make comments, or pay a compliment. Remember, the focus is on networking. A successful networking situation leads to further contact. This does not refer to sales calls to people with whom you already have a relationship, in which case you would be asking questions that identify problems, needs, and concerns. As you become more experienced in conversational skills, you will find that many of the questions you ask in a sales call can be used in networking situations to identify the quality of the contact. The purpose here, however, is to address how to initiate a contact, build rapport, and present yourself in a favorable manner during those brief encounters when you are mingling or networking.

KEEPING THE CONVERSATION GOING

There are many techniques for moving conversation to other subjects or more in-depth detail. The following should help organize your thoughts and keep a conversation going.

■ Use self-disclosure.

"I was just reading about . . ."

"That reminds me of . . ."

"We're refinishing our deck and I'd sure like to find . . ."

"I'm very interested in learning about benchmarking. Have you . . .?"

■ Expand the topic.

"How interesting. Tell me more."

"What's the story behind . . .?"

"What do you mean by . . .?"

■ Move from the general to the specific.

"Would you give me an example of what you mean by that?"

"How does that industry trend affect your business?"

■ Move from the specific to the general.

> "What impact will that have on the project?"

> "How do you plan to get buy-in from the rest of the team?"

■ Go from the present to the future.

> "What will you do next?"

> "What will that look like down the road?"

■ Go from the present to the past.

> "What happened first?"

> "What led up to that decision?"

■ Focus on similarities and differences.

> "Have you been through something like this before?"

> "Which traits do you find desirable?"

> "What other novelists do you find interesting?"

■ Look for extremes and contrasts.

> "What's the downside?"

> "What's the best thing that could happen?"

■ Bring up the unusual, the outrageous.

> "If you could have lunch with anyone living or dead, who might that be?"

> "If time and money weren't an issue, what would you do for a vacation?"

ENDING THE CONVERSATION

Bringing a conversation to a conclusion also makes people uneasy. We are often afraid to leave for fear of making the other person feel bad. Yet you do not want to walk away without bringing the conversation to a close. The goal is to close off the conversation without closing the relationship.

■ Return to your goals for the event.

> "I promised myself to find someone tonight who is working with the new accounting software I just got. It was nice to meet you."

"I vowed when I came today to meet two more bankers before I leave. Please excuse me while I pursue this goal."

"I'm desperate to find someone who knows of a good electrician. If you hear of anyone, please point me out to them."

■ Take your leave.

"I want to go speak to the membership chairman."

"I'm going to circulate and meet some of the other CPAs."

"My stomach says that it's time to sample the hors d'oeuvres."

■ Be inviting.

"I'd like to talk to the speaker. Would you care to join me?"

"Would you like to browse the exhibits with me?"

"I see the executive director. Would you like to meet her?"

■ Ask for help.

"Do you know someone here I could talk to about joining that task force?"

"I hoped to meet someone with experience detecting fraud. Do you know of anyone here?"

"Would you introduce me to one of the members who is using that new operating system?"

■ Show appreciation.

"I've enjoyed hearing about your family reunion."

"I'm glad you introduced me to the subject of international mutual funds. Thank you."

"It was so nice to meet you and have the chance to talk."

■ Continue the relationship.

"I'd like to follow up with that. Would you mind if I give you a call?"

"Since you enjoy walking too, would you like to join me sometime?"

"I have a great article on that. I'll send you a copy."

"I don't want to monopolize your time tonight. May I call you to arrange to meet later?"

"Give me a call next week. Here's my card."

Once you have begun the leave-taking process, do not linger. Offer your hand for a handshake, thank the person, and move on. The conversation may have ended, but you have done your best to keep the relationship alive.

It is important to remember that good conversational skills are just that—skills. With time, patience, and practice, you will find that your conversational savvy is a strong personal marketing tool.

■ ■ ■

Keep the following icebreaker questions in mind in case all else fails.

■ If you could have lunch with anyone living or dead, who would that be and why?

■ I have always been interested in what people do in their spare time. Which hobbies or activities do you enjoy?

■ If time and money were not a concern, where would you go on vacation?

■ What is your favorite kind of vacation?

■ Where is your favorite place to spend time alone?

■ Who were your heroes when you were a child?

■ Tell me about the best gift you have ever received?

■ Of all the places you have lived, which is your favorite?

■ If you had five minutes to evacuate your home, what would you take with you?

■ Which movie have you seen many times?

■ Have you read any good books lately?"

ENTERTAINING AND HOSTING AS BUSINESS SKILLS

"A host is like a general: it takes a mishap to reveal his genius."

—Horace

"Make everything as simple as possible, but not more so."

—Albert Einstein

A few years ago, I conducted a seminar on dining and hosting skills at a private club for members. After the luncheon and lecture was finished, a prominent lawyer in his early forties approached me. He commented that he had realized during the lecture on hosting skills that whenever he and his wife entertain at home, he becomes a guest. It had not occurred to him that the responsibility for hosting the evening was his as much as his wife's. His guests expected him to be their host, only to find that he did not fill the role very well.

Entertaining is an extension of the way you conduct yourself professionally at the office. When done with style, with a concern for the guest, and with attention to detail, business entertaining is an art. And it requires the mastery of certain basic skills.

For this chapter, and in discussing entertaining and the skill of hosting, I would like to expand the definition of hosting to include more than entertaining in the common sense of the word. When you think of hosting, include any event that brings a person on your turf—in your office or home or at an event you or your firm planned. Appropriate guest behavior is called for at any time that you are on someone else's turf, or are attending an event they planned.

If, in your role as president of your state society chapter, you think of yourself as the host of all the chapter meetings, I guarantee that the attendees will feel more welcomed and willing to participate.

If you and your firm are planning an informational lecture or seminar and you see yourselves as the hosts, I can guarantee that the participants—whether clients, potential clients, or referral sources—will feel a stronger bond and attraction.

If you welcome a visitor into your office as a gracious host, I can guarantee that the visitor will feel important and comfortable.

If you take a client or two to lunch, and exhibit the appropriate behaviors for a host, I can guarantee the business at hand will proceed with more ease.

Everything I have observed over more than a decade of speaking and advising on manners, dining, and hosting skills points to one conclusion: If you see yourself as a host or hostess, you will think of the people coming into your home or office as guests or visitors. And the more you think of these people as guests, the more your behavior and attitude shifts and transforms you into an experienced host or hostess.

GRACIOUSNESS: THE KEYNOTE

The word *gracious* comes up frequently when talking about hosting. One of the exercises in my workshops centers around this word. I ask the class to think of other words associated with it, and the words that come to mind include kind, considerate, polite, well-mannered, cultured, thoughtful, humble, appreciative, poised, self-assured, and accommodating. Then I ask the participants to think of someone they consider to be gracious. Next, I ask them to describe how they *feel* when they are in the presence of this gracious person. Words such as special, important, valued, comfortable, at ease, listened to, and appreciated are always mentioned.

A gracious person has the ability to put others at ease and make them feel valued. This skill is critical to effective entertaining and hosting. In fact, gracious behavior is effective in all human relations. It does not mean you cannot be a tough, effective negotiator or businessperson. It means that showing others respect and treating them with dignity is a principle that guides all your behavior and is a skill that can always be put to use.

HOSTING ERRORS

The following are the most frequent hosting mistakes. Paying special attention to these behaviors will help you enjoy entertaining more as you become a more confident and self-assured host.

Hosting Error Number 1—Failure to Think of Clients or Visitors as Guests

If you fail to see your clients as guests when they visit your offices, there is a good chance you will fail to think of yourself as a host. This oversight in turn affects expectations and attitudes. Let me give you an example.

A management consultant, doing client satisfaction research for a major accounting firm's West Coast office, called one of the firm's clients in New York for feedback. During the interview, the consultant found out the client was very satisfied with the work of the firm. The client felt the work was excellent, the value good, and the fees fair. But he mentioned that the last time he was in San Francisco, he had promised himself that he would find another accounting firm if he had to take himself out to dinner one more time.

The problem was that the client felt unappreciated by the CPA firm. The firm's partners, on the other hand, assumed that this long-time client, who had been to San Francisco many times, was comfortable in the city, and that he had formed his preferences in restaurants, museums, and hotels. The partners neglected their hosting responsibilities to the detriment of their business relationship with this client.

It is especially important to see yourself as a host in your offices in the following instances.

■ A higher ranking person from within the firm or company and one you seldom see comes by your office.

- You have an appointment with a client, or anyone else.
- You are interviewing students and showing them around.

Hosting Error Number 2—Failure to Give Clear and Complete Instructions

It is the host's responsibility to communicate instructions and directions and to guide guests. In a common mixup, the host is waiting at one restaurant while the client is at another restaurant with a similar name. For example, one CPA found herself sitting in a restaurant with her regional manager while her clients waited for her at their office. It had always been this woman's habit to provide her clients with transportation to and from the restaurants, but on this occasion she left a message explaining a change in the routine. Unfortunately, she failed to speak with the clients directly to confirm the plans, and her message was lost or misunderstood.

If you meet a guest in the reception area, you—the host—lead the way to the office. Some hallways are narrow and cannot accommodate people walking side-by-side. You should reassure the guest with directions such as, "We'll be turning right at this next hallway," or "My office is the next door on our left."

It is always courteous to walk your guest back to the reception area after your meeting. Any number of people have gotten lost by taking a wrong turn in an unfamiliar office complex.

Once a client is in your office, offer to take his or her umbrella, or to hang up his or her coat and any other outer garments. If you do not have a place for these items, indicate to the guest that it is okay to put them on an extra chair. Otherwise, the guest should keep all belongings in the chair in which he or she is sitting.

If it is appropriate, offer your guest coffee, tea, soda, or seltzer. If the guest accepts a beverage, be sure to have a beverage yourself. You do not have to drink it; the point of the gesture is that you do not want your guest to drink alone. It is also your responsibility to indicate seating, which leads us to the next error commonly made by hosts.

Hosting Error Number 3—Failure to Think Out the Seating in Advance

Many of you, more than once, have found yourself in the following situation. You are at a friend's house for dinner. After cocktails and hors d'oeuvres, the host asks everyone to move into the dining room for dinner. You all go into the dining room and stand there. Finally, some brave soul asks the host where he or she wants everyone to sit. The host replies, "Oh, anywhere is fine." And everyone continues to stand around, feeling a bit uncomfortable with this lack of direction.

When you are in someone else's home or office, it is inappropriate to take a seat without permission. Even though it is implied that the host wants you to take a seat, the gracious guest will always wait to have seating indicated first.

If you are taking one or more people to lunch, it is your responsibility as host to indicate seating there as well. The guest of honor, usually the client, takes the seat of honor. That generally is the chair that the maître d' pulls out first. You would indicate verbally to the main client that you would like him or her to sit there. You would then indicate to the guest who is second in rank the chair you want him or her to take.

Beware of making assumptions based on gender, which is usually irrelevant. For example, a staff accountant once told me about a serious mistake she made when she lunched with one of her firm's partners and two male clients. When the maître d' showed them to their table, he pulled a chair out, and she immediately sat in it, assuming it was for the "lady." Afterward, the partner admonished her. Not only had she failed to wait for his—the host's—direction, she also took the "seat of honor," which should have gone to the most important client.

This story makes two points. First, always wait for direction from your host. If you are the host, indicate where you would like your guests to sit. Second, notice how the rules of etiquette have changed to accommodate the business environment. Social etiquette is based on chivalry, which is gender based. Business etiquette, on the other hand, is based on hierarchy, status, rank or position, not gender.

Seating can have great significance and should not be taken lightly. In restaurants, the bench (banquette) seating is considered the prime seat because it usually looks out into the rest of the dining area. If you have serious business topics to discuss, you may not want your guest facing the main dining area with all its distractions. If the discussions are confidential in nature, you may want your primary guest sitting on your right, adjacent to your seat. Otherwise, most people like to be in full view of their guest to be able to watch body language as well. In this case, the guest would be seated on the opposite side of the table from you. If you are entertaining two people, have the primary guest sit across from you, with the secondary one on your left.

If you are involved with international guests, you will want to take seating very seriously. Follow protocol and cater to the most important guest.

Hosting Error Number 4—Failure to Make Introductions Properly

The ability to make introductions properly and with ease is an important business skill. People feel uncomfortable talking with someone they do not know. Introductions, whether introducing the receptionist to a new client, or your spouse to the managing partner, pave the way for conversation and help build rapport. How you make introductions shows respect. Chapter 10, "Meeting and Greeting People," goes into more detail about the correct way to make introductions.

At larger functions, such as an open house, meeting, or an informational seminar, introductions are equally important. Even though name tags are usually provided, those hosting the event should make sure everyone has been introduced to at least one other person.

Hosting Error Number 5—Failure to Pace the Meeting or Meal

If you called the meeting or set up the business lunch, it is your responsibility to start the event on time, keep it moving, and end on time. Pacing shows respect for people's time, and is expected of hosts.

In a restaurant, you usually have several opportunities to communicate with the serving staff, which allows you to influence the pace of the meal. For example, if you do not have a lot of time for lunch, you might ask the server to point out the menu items that take extra time to prepare. This question indicates to the server that you are on a tight time schedule.

During a business lunch, conversation can move from small talk to business after the orders are taken or as soon as the food arrives. Again, it is the responsibility of the host, not the guest, to bring up business.

If someone overstays a visit to your office, it is appropriate to bring the conversation or business at hand to a close. You can say, "John, I'd like to hear more about that, but I have a project on deadline that I need to attend to." Stand, walk around your desk to the door, and escort the person out. If the person is a client, see them to the reception area or the elevators. Thank them for their time.

Hosting Error Number 6—Failure to Control the Conversation

A saying sums it up: Those who talk dominate conversation. Those who listen and ask questions control communication.

Tom Olsen, while working for American President Lines, learned the importance of this the hard way. Several years ago, he was a country manager living in Tokyo. He decided to entertain clients one weekend and invited two expatriates and their spouses to dinner. During cocktails, the conversation turned to the upcoming Unites States Presidential election. One of the couples was a zealous Republican, the other an equally zealous Democrat. Within a short time, the discussion became so heated that one couple got up and stomped out, leaving a very embarrassed and dismayed host.

Nevertheless, the burden of guiding this conversation was on the host. Once it became apparent that the topic was triggering emotions, he would have been wise to interrupt with a comment like, "I know how important this election is to everyone, but tonight is meant to be festive. You will never guess what happened to me the other day when ..."

There are many situations in which you, as a host, can defuse tension with all the wonderful stories and anecdotes that you have learned to keep in mind. For example, suppose you overhear disparaging remarks being made by an employee or a guest at a function hosted by your firm. You could interrupt by taking the person aside or by interjecting a new topic. Small dinner parties held in your home may present similar problems. If a conversation veers off and excludes guests who are unable to participate or simply not interested, you can be a good host by changing the subject to a topic that includes everyone.

Hosting Error Number 7—Failure to Display Good Table Manners

Table manners are a gift you give to those with whom you dine. In fact, more hiring decisions are made at a meal today than ever before. Even entry-level job applicants are being taken to breakfast or lunch before the hiring decision is made. The reason? People assume that if you have table manners, you were taught manners in general and have good social skills. Conversely, if you have poor table manners, the assumption is that you lack social skills. Employers cannot afford to hire anyone who is badly socialized because it affects the relationships that person has with fellow employees and their clients.

You want to avoid embarrassing yourself or your firm with poor table manners. For more information on appropriate table manners for a business person, turn to appendix C, "Table Manners for the Business Professional." Since you eat every day, you have every chance to practice until your eating habits are correct and polished.

THE VALUE OF ENTERTAINING

Entertaining is a powerful business tool. Business entertaining is a multimillion-dollar industry because companies have found that it is good business to entertain clients, colleagues, civic and political leaders, associates, referral sources, suppliers, and potential customers. Every business or social function holds the potential for creating goodwill. It does not matter whether it is fried chicken and potato salad at a picnic, or champagne and exquisite hors d'oeuvres at an art gallery. Usually, the relaxed atmosphere makes it easy for people to get to know each other, paving the way for future business connections.

The success of any event—whether it is lunch with an important client, an open house held for the firm, or an invitation to a sports event—depends on careful planning, attention to detail, and the host's demonstrated concern for every guest. At small events, such as a lunch attended by only two or three people, it is essential to make each guest feel like an important dignitary. Similarly, at an open house, each guest should be made to feel special. Big events pose a different problem: It is possible for a guest attending a large function to never get to meet the host or anyone from the firm because there are so many people and so much going on. Nevertheless, good planning can prevent these lapses of graciousness.

WHY DO LUNCH?

You are probably aware that more business is conducted over food than at the boardroom table. Going to lunch with clients or associates gives you the opportunity for all the following.

- Meet with them one-on-one.
- Talk shop.
- Make a good impression by showing your capabilities and skills.
- Build rapport and get to know them better.
- Nurture an existing relationship.
- Repay a kindness or favor.
- Celebrate a sale, a promotion, the signing of a contract, an award, or a birthday.
- Embellish your image and the image of your company.
- Simply be nice.

Since businesspeople spend so much time together at the table eating, drinking, and talking shop, it is important to know how to handle yourself properly at the table. If you are not worrying about the food or your table manners, you can focus on the people and the business at hand. Your understanding of the nuances of dining etiquette also demonstrates your attention to detail—something any employee would want to develop as an integral part of staying competitive.

Let's explore some of the events and functions important to business development.

THE BUSINESS MEAL

There are several stages to every successful meal. Each has its own set of rules and requires thought and planning to run smoothly.

Extending the Invitation

When you extend the invitation, mention the reason. Be clear about why you want to take this person to lunch. If you want to ask for advice, explore a referral relationship, or reciprocate a favor, you would want to explain. Why? Because time is valuable and most businesspeople do not want to spend time having lunch with every person who asks.

For example, you might tell people that you are interested in learning more about the key issues and major players in the construction industry. If they have time, they may be willing to go to lunch to share this information. However, if time is tight, they can then recommend someone else who may be of more help to you. Making it clear to your guests why you are extending the invitation gives them the opportunity to—

■ Choose to handle it over the phone if they prefer.

■ Indicate that they cannot help you.

■ Prepare ahead if necessary.

■ Decline if they believe that the invitation may not warrant the time involved.

I get calls almost weekly from people who want to get together to have me explain to them how to get started in the speaking business, or how to start a consulting business. If I took the time to lunch with all these people, I would have no time for my work. I have also learned from experience that most people are not willing to do the homework needed to go out on their own. So, I usually ask a few questions about the research they have already done. Small Business Association classes? Books? Seminars? Most have done nothing. My solution is to give them some homework and ask them to call me afterward if they still have questions. Most never call again. Those that do are serious. For these individuals, I usually arrange a telephone interview, rather than lunch. It saves time.

If it is part of your personal marketing strategy to have lunch at least once a week with someone in your professional network, keep the following guidelines in mind.

■ Extend the invitation three to five days ahead whenever possible.

■ Call the person yourself to extend the invitation and to confirm on the day of the lunch.

■ If you reach voice mail, leave a complete message so the person can respond appropriately.

■ Verify whether or not you will meet at the restaurant or pick up the person.

■ Give clear and concise directions for the location of the restaurant and time of meal.

■ Communicate appropriate attire (some clubs require ties).

Choosing the Restaurant

For lunch to go well, you will want your choice to be appropriate. Keep in mind the points that are addressed in the following sections.

Deciding Where to Go

Never ask your guests where they would like to go. Offer either a choice of two restaurants or no choice at all. Perhaps you belong to a private club and want to make sure you can sign for the tab. If you give your guests a choice, you might say, "Would you like to meet at the Metropolitan Grill [which is close to their offices] or at McCormick's Fish House [which has a wider variety of foods]?" If the guests do not care, then make the decision immediately yourself.

Knowing Your Options

Frequent several restaurants where you know the menu and the staff. Different occasions call for various atmospheres. A meal over which you want to discuss business will not go well in a noisy deli. Since you may want to impress someone, a private club would be more appropriate.

Weighing All Factors

The following is a list of specifics about restaurants that will help you make the right choice:

- Menu, price, and kind of food
- Parking
- Location and distance to travel
- Ambiance, mood, and noise level
- Your familiarity with the menu, layout, and staff

Hosting

Hosting is where you can shine. Gracious hosting requires paying attention to details. No matter who you are taking to lunch—a new client, a colleague, or an established referral source—you will want to practice your hosting skills, which can include the following, until they become positive habits.

Timing

Arriving early will give you plenty of time to do the following.

- Make arrangements for paying the bill before your guests arrive. This is a graceful way to establish with the restaurant staff that you are the host, and prevents any later confusion about who is paying. (This practice can be especially useful for a woman or young person taking an older, more experienced person out for lunch or dinner.)

■ Take your guests' coats and check them. As the host, you pay for this service.

■ Wait for everyone to arrive before going to your table. If, however, you know beforehand that someone is going to be late, it is acceptable for you and your party to be seated.

■ If you are seated while you are waiting for your guests to arrive, do not disturb the table settings or the bread and crackers. You want the table presentation to be at its best when others arrive. Nevertheless, you may order a beverage or sip your water.

■ Think out the seating arrangement ahead of time. If there are more than two people in your party, the guest of honor sits on your right, because you are the host.

■ Indicate to your guests where each of them should sit, and make sure that they are seated before you sit down.

Setting the Pace

It is up to the host, not the guests, to move the topic of conversation from small talk to the business at hand, usually after the order has been taken or when the food arrives. In addition, do the following.

■ Communicate with the serving staff any time constraints.

■ Be respectful of the time and pace the meal accordingly.

■ If you are a fast eater, slow down; if you are a slow eater, pick up your pace, leave some food, or order less.

Ordering Food and Beverages

As a host, you should always guide the placing of orders as follows.

■ Have your guests give their orders first.

■ If your guests order beverages, you should too, although your order need not be alcoholic.

■ Coffee and tea, which inhibit the taste buds, should follow a meal (except breakfast).

■ When guests ask you to recommend items on the menu, their question may veil their concern about prices. If the cost is not a concern, suggest several items that span the range of prices on the menu. If you would want to contain the cost of the meal, recommend items that fall within the range that you prefer.

■ Avoid foods that are messy or unfamiliar because they can become a distraction during the meal.

■ Business and alcohol make a poor combination that is much less accepted than in the past. Moderate the alcohol consumption of all business-related meals.

■ If wine is appropriate, do not hesitate to ask the server or wine steward for a recommendation; they know which wines go best with side dishes as well as the entrees. Indicate your preferred price range.

■ Ask your guests what their preferences are in wine. Note that wine drinking no longer follows strict convention; some people drink white wine with everything, and others always drink red wine.

■ Do not order more courses than your guests; eating alone in front of others is ungracious and awkward.

Picking Up the Tab

A basic rule is: Whoever extends the invitation picks up the tab. Above all, however, payment should be handled discreetly, according to the following.

■ If the guest is a senior, or a prominent person who insists on paying, do not argue. Reciprocate on a later occasion.

■ Have your money or credit card handy to avoid fumbling. If the bill is handed to you on a tray or folder, place your cash or card inside but so that part of it is visible; this allows the transaction to unfold smoothly.

■ Handle any discrepancies or problems away from the table and your guests.

Tipping

Tipping, also the host's responsibility, should also be handled with discretion. Keep in mind the following basics so that they become second nature.

■ Tip on the *un*taxed portion of the bill.

■ Extra service by the wine steward or maître d' can be figured separately and indicated on the charge slip.

■ Tip 15 to 18 percent for lunch, 15 to 20 percent for dinner, and more for exceptional service.

■ Carry one-dollar bills and quarters to easily tip for coat checking, parking attendants, and so on.

Handling Mishaps

Another responsibility of the good host is to graciously smooth over anything that goes amiss. The following are tips for how to handle problems.

- Cancel or change the date only if absolutely necessary.
- If a guest is a no-show, call his or her office after fifteen minutes.
- Wait thirty to forty minutes, then either order or leave after explaining the situation to the server and tipping accordingly.
- Be attentive to your guests' orders to make sure they have been given what they asked for. If the steak is well done but medium rare was ordered, it is your duty to bring the problem to the attention of the server.
- If the service is extremely poor, there is no need to discuss it with your guests, other than to make a comment such as, "The service is not up to their usual standards, today. I'm sorry."
- The host calls the server or table captain to the table.
- Complain to management out of earshot of your guests.
- If there is a spill on clothing, ask to have club soda brought to the table. Do not use water to dab on the spot.
- If you suffer from a sneezing or coughing fit, or a nose bleed, excuse yourself from the table.

OTHER HOSTED EVENTS

Many times throughout your professional career, you will be involved in planning open houses, seminars, classes, and celebratory functions designed to include clients, referral sources, media, potential clients, and others from the business community.

Guidelines for Smoothly Running Events

Why are some events more successful than others? Usually, it is the planning and attention to detail that will make the difference. The key is to remember it is a hosted function, so make sure you and every other company host understand that you are expected to make certain all guests feel special. Be sure that the following arrangements are made ahead of time.

- Invitations are sent out far enough in advance so guests can arrange their schedules in order to attend.
- An interesting mix of people attend, including new faces.
- Company personnel are trained to be gracious hosts who greet guests, take care of coats and outer wraps, offer name tags, introduce guests to each other, and direct everyone to the food and beverages.

■ If background music is played, it should be soft enough to allow conversation.

■ If the event calls for tables and chairs, enough are provided.

■ The room is not overcrowded and hot.

■ The hosts circulate to welcome as many people as possible.

■ The event ends on time.

The way you behave in public strongly affects your image and the image of the company you represent. At events or meetings planned by you or your firm, it is important to know how to behave properly in order to build and nurture the relationships of those attending. It is the time you put your best foot forward to make a good impression.

Meetings With Presentations

Many meetings or functions include a speaker or presentation by one or more people. The following will keep distractions to a minimum and assure the success of the presentation.

■ If either you or someone else is a speaker, make sure someone is also designated to introduce the speaker(s)—with a prepared introduction, not something off the cuff. Let each speaker know when they will start, and more important, exactly when they should end.

■ Test all audiovisual equipment and lighting beforehand.

■ Try out the microphone and sound system ahead of time to make sure everything works and that there is no feedback or screechy sounds.

■ Make sure all handouts, workbooks, or presentation materials are correct and clean, and there are enough to distribute to all present.

If the event is an educational seminar or informational meeting and you have invited clients, potential clients, colleagues that refer business, and others from the community, remember to attend to the following very important details.

■ Have someone from the firm personally greet every person attending.

■ Make sure everyone has a name tag that clearly states his or her name and company.

■ Designate hosts for every table. (That means that employees do not sit together. Instead, each hosts a table in order to make sure that everyone has met the others at the table.)

■ Make sure everyone from the firm has business cards handy and uses them properly.

Most of this seems like common business sense. However, it is not. A few years ago I was called by a marketing director for an East Coast office of one of the Big Six accounting firms. Her firm had just held an informational meeting with less than stellar results. It was possible for a potential client to come in, sit down, listen, and leave, without ever meeting anyone from the firm. She felt they had lost the opportunity to nurture some of their contacts and competitors' clients because no one took hosting the event seriously. The managing partner felt that passing out business cards was passé, and did not see a need to make sure each table was hosted by a CPA. He felt the reputation of the firm and the timeliness of the information could stand on its own. A great marketing opportunity was missed.

THE FLIP SIDE: BEING A GRACIOUS GUEST

Just as there are expectations of the host, there are also expectations for guests. Whether you are in a client's office, the guest of a banker at a theater event, attending an open house, or in someone's home, you need to know and practice appropriate behavior.

Responding to Invitations

Often, the first part of being a guest is to respond to an invitation. Keep the following in mind.

- Written invitations should always be answered, whether or not an RSVP is requested. Answering invitations is a good habit, and your thoughtfulness will be noticed. (A common complaint from hosts is that so few people answer invitations, including invitations for functions held by their own companies; even partners fail to respond to invitations to retreats.)

- Respond to all invitations within seven days.

- Do not assume that any invitation is for two and that you are free to bring along your spouse, or a friend or coworker. If you are unsure, ask.

- If, at the last minute, you cannot attend, *always* call and inform your host. Do this for all events, dinners, or outings. It is thoughtful and courteous.

Read the Cues

Your host will guide you through the event. Take your cues from his or her signals and their nuances. Observe the following in order to be a good guest.

■ Even in someone's office, do not take a seat until your host invites you to do so.

■ Keep your coat and other personal belongings with you unless you are invited to do otherwise. Drape outerwear on the back of the chair you are sitting in. Do not spread out.

■ Be sensitive to when it is time to leave. Listen and watch for signals from your host that the event is coming to a close.

Dining Out as a Guest

In restaurants, be a considerate and gracious guest by keeping the following in mind.

■ Be on time.

■ If you arrive ahead of your host, wait in the restaurant lobby or reception area, unless you are asked to do otherwise.

■ Wait to be seated by your host. This is especially important if you are younger or more junior than other guests. Gender is usually irrelevant.

■ Unless your host encourages you to do otherwise, do not order any of the more expensive items on the menu. In the same spirit, do not order several courses unless the host encourages you to do so.

■ Do not order courses such as salad, soup, or dessert that no one else is ordering, so as not to disrupt the pace of the meal.

■ Do not sip beverages or begin eating until either the host or guest of honor has begun or until the host has invited everyone to do so.

■ Pace your eating to match the others.

■ Send a short thank-you note to your host within three to five days. Do so in writing unless you know the person very well.

■ If something at your place setting is tainted (for example, there is a hair or insect in your food), handle the situation in light of your relationship with the host. The most tactful response is to simply not eat or drink the unacceptable item, but say nothing about it. If you cannot do this without being noticed, or if you are comfortable enough with your host, mention the problem to him or her. Let the host call the situation to the attention of the server. The last resort, if it seems appropriate, is to quietly and inconspicuously speak to the server yourself.

■ Do not complain about smoke, allergies, or any other disamenities. If you cannot eat something that is served, simply do not eat it. If anyone asks why, just say the item does not agree with you.

GIFT GIVING

Giving gifts creates goodwill, nurtures relationships, and pleases the recipient when done with sensitivity and imagination. The opportunity or occasion to buy gifts for clients, suppliers, associates, behind-the-scenes people who help out, employees, and other service personnel comes up frequently. The reason may be any of the following:

- To show appreciation
- To acknowledge and celebrate a special occasion
- To cement a friendship or business relationship
- To apologize
- To congratulate someone for an award or other achievement
- To curry favor for yourself or your company

When giving gifts, it is important to keep the following in mind.

- Always present them wrapped or attractively packaged.
- Keep them appropriate for the occasion and the person—neither too expensive nor too personal.
- Check on company policies; many companies do not allow employees to accept gifts of any kind.
- When appropriate, select a gift that can be shared, such as candy, fruit, cookies, flavored popcorn or plants.
- Present gifts in person whenever possible.
- Be observant throughout the year and note details, such as interests, colors, reading material, foods, and pictures that will help make your gift selections personal and meaningful.
- Enclose a card, note, or your business card.

Gift giving need not be a difficult process, especially if you make observations and keep notes on clients and associates. And remember, it is not the expense, but rather the thoughtfulness that people appreciate.

THANK-YOU NOTES AND OTHER ACKNOWLEDGMENTS

Keep your pen and note cards handy. Tom Peters, in his latest book, *The Pursuit of WOW!*, considers the following the most important piece of advice he gives in his book: Don't forget your thank-you notes!

Become a stickler for expressing your appreciation, and put it in writing. People respond positively to being acknowledged and tend to not forget a kindness. This gesture will do more than you can imagine to build positive relationships with coworkers, employees, service personnel, clients, referral sources, and others in your personal network.

124

The power of a thank-you note is hard to beat. Positive reinforcement goes a long way and most people do not give (or get) much of it. Writing a note (as opposed to a phone call, which is good, too), demonstrates a level of effort and it leaves behind something permanent. The note does not even have to be more than two or three sentences long.

When should you express appreciation? A thank-you note can acknowledge the following, which are only examples:

- Good ideas shared at staff meetings
- Timely reports
- Favors done
- Referrals
- People willing to chair committees
- Those who have influenced you in some way
- Strong role models and mentors
- Those who put in extra time and effort
- Leaders willing to take risks or have the buck stop at their desks

Do not pass up any opportunity to write a note of appreciation. You will be amazed, even years later, at the response. It is a sure way to distinguish yourself in the marketplace as well.

■ ■ ■

Keep the following in mind when developing the art of business entertaining.

- The goal of hosting is to put your guests at ease and make them feel comfortable.
- If you are hosting international clients, remember that the rest of the world is much more formal than the United States. Civility is expected.
- Extend invitations personally whenever you can.
- Always RSVP within a week of receiving an invitation.
- Do not assume the invitation includes a guest. Ask if you are unsure.
- Seat the guest of honor on the host's right.
- Reconfirm the arrangements with both the restaurant and the guest the day before.
- At large events, do not wait to be introduced; introduce yourself.
- When making a toast, keep it short, simple and appropriate.
- Stay seated and do not drink when being toasted.
- Always respond to a toast.
- Watch your host or those more senior for guidance as to when to start eating or drinking.

- Dress appropriately, whether at the theater, sporting event, or in someone's home. Ask if you are wondering about what is appropriate.
- Turn off your pager or cellular phone at events. Do not take calls when you are entertaining or being entertained.
- Remember that table hopping is often considered rude and inconsiderate.
- When you are hosting large events, plan to have someone greet every guest.
- Always maintain your professionalism, even when entertaining clients who have become friends.

MEETING

AND

GREETING

PEOPLE

*"You never get a second chance to
make a good first impression."*

—Author Unknown

Sales can be made or lost, careers enhanced or destroyed, opportunities offered or lost, and relationships established or broken—all in the fleeting few minutes of a first impression. In our culture, major lasting judgments are made based on our first impression of others. Every day we make first impressions in meetings, briefings, interviews, chance encounters, sales calls, and the myriad of encounters of our daily business life.

First impressions include everything people notice first: posture, facial expressions, physical appearance, eye contact, and the tone of voice. As a professional, you want the first impression of you to be positive, in order to increase the likelihood that your message will be heard.

Your ability to meet and greet people starts with understanding your image and how it influences others' perception. Paying attention to small but important details can help you make friends and influence others. Making a good first impression every time enhances your self-confidence, credibility, and impact on others.

THE CRITICAL FIRST IMPRESSION

Social psychologists tell us that on first meeting, people instantly make judgments about other people, sometimes only subconsciously. That *first impression* is most often visual, and it crystallizes before you have uttered even a word.

Whenever we wait at the airport, stand in line at the supermarket, spend time at a Chamber of Commerce function, or attend a conference, we observe others. No doubt, you make judgments about people based solely on *watching* them. We all do this and we can all learn from the process. Why does one person *look* educated or more powerful? Why does another person *look* like they lack confidence?

Over the years, you learn to read a person's clothing, appearance, expressions, and gestures. It is a silent language, a visual shorthand, and it helps you form your subjective decisions about the other person's honesty, background, friendliness, attitude, and intent.

Anyone you meet may form a first impression of you inside ten seconds. Nevertheless, the attention span and powers of retention of most people are greatest during the first few minutes. Be aware that in those first few minutes, a viewer or other person will arrive at a conclusions about ten of your personal characteristics, as follows, based on your *clothing alone*:

- Economic level
- Educational level
- Trustworthiness
- Social position

- Level of sophistication
- Economic background
- Social background
- Educational background
- Level of success
- Moral character

Remember the old saying about not judging a book by its cover? On the contrary, publishers have long known that an attractive cover will indeed influence a person to at least pick up the book and give it a glance. This is true about people, too.

First, people focus on what they see, generally in the following sequence:

1. Skin color
2. Gender
3. Age
4. Appearance
5. Facial expressions
6. Eye contact
7. Movement
8. Personal space
9. Touch

Although you can do little to alter the first three attributes, you have control over the others.

Second, others then tend to focus on what they hear. This part of first impressions is based on the following voice characteristics:

- Tone
- Volume
- Pitch
- Rate
- Quality
- Articulation

Third and last, people then focus on the words they hear and their meaning.[16] It is not that what a person says is unimportant, but if others

---

[16] Albert Mehrabian. *Nonverbal Communication*. Chicago: Aldine-Atherton, 1972.

cannot get past what that person looks like or are stopped by the way the person sounds, they may not care what that person has to say. For example, you may be known for your expertise, but that is not what people focus on first.

SELLING YOURSELF NONVERBALLY

It is much easier to sell your products and services if you have sold yourself successfully as being credible, trustworthy, and a person of integrity. Because silent communication has such a profound impact on effective communication, silent signals and what they mean are important.

Research conducted by Dr. Albert Mehrabian in the early 1970s has made us painfully aware of the tremendous impact that nonverbal communication has on the way we are perceived. His research showed that the verbal part of any message accounted for only 7 percent of the impact, while the nonverbal part, voice (38 percent) and the physical appearance (55 percent), accounted for 93 percent of the total impact. His research proved that our total impact, when communicating one-on-one in nontechnical situations, comes from the following three basic components of human behavior:

1. The message, meaning what is said and its content
2. The voice, including rate of speaking, volume, articulation, quality, and pitch
3. Physical appearance, including facial expression, eye movement, gestures, posture, dress, and grooming

As a business professional, you want to communicate effectively and not send the wrong messages by your nonverbal cues. Paying attention to what influences first impressions gives you a communication edge.

When you first meet someone, you tend to engage all your senses for a longer period of time, and pay more attention to them. This is one of the reasons first impressions are so lasting and hard to change. As a result, it is important to control your nonverbal communication when first meeting people. Generally, you want to showcase your attributes, sending the message of confidence, credibility, and trustworthiness. In order to do so, pay attention to the nonverbal cues outlined in chart 10-1 when meeting and greeting others for the first time.

CHART 10-1: NONVERBAL BEHAVIORS

OBSERVABLE BEHAVIORS	DO'S	DON'TS
Eye Contact	Greet the person with your eyes.	Do not avoid eye contact, gaze around room or over shoulders.
Facial Expressions	Express enjoyment at meeting them, put on a pleasant face, smile.	Do not look bored or disinterested.
Movement	Stand and move purposefully toward the person for the handshake.	Do not remain seated, shuffle, or make jerky movements toward the person.
Posture	Stand tall and confidently.	Do not slouch or slump.
Touch	Shake hands with medium-firm pressure, connecting where thumb webs meet.	Do not offer fingers, the back of your hand, or limp pressure.
Vocal Cues	Sound interested and enthused in a calm manner.	Do not speak rapidly, loudly, or use a monotone pitch. Do not sound bored.

Remember that your nonverbal behaviors tell others a lot about you. In initial interactions people "read" your nonverbal cues and make assumptions and judgments about you.

- Your facial expressions are considered an indicator of your mood, attitude, and personality. Faces express basic emotions.
- Your willingness to make eye contact reflects self-confidence, shows respect, and indicates you are listening.
- Posture and body movement tend to communicate power and status. The way you move shows your responsiveness and willingness to build rapport.
- The voice may be the single most important nonverbal determinant of credibility, as perceived by others. The development of personal credibility requires the development of a confident voice.
- A person's physical impression reflects their respect for themselves, their job, their profession, and their associates.

132

In business, we are often in situations where selling our abilities is important. More likely than not, we must sell ourselves to a potential client or employer before he or she will buy from us or consider hiring us. Therefore, it is very important to pay attention to the *effect* of your appearance on others, especially when first meeting people.

Successful people tend to consider the ability to manage nonverbal behaviors as critical. In turn, people who are sensitive to nonverbal behaviors are perceived as better adjusted, more extroverted, more popular, more effective in interpersonal relationships, and better listeners. In addition, be sensitive to the nonverbal clues that you send because nonverbal communication—

1. Is the first and biggest source of the first impression in face-to-face interactions.

2. Is the yardstick against which your words and actions are measured.

3. Precedes and frames all communication.

4. Tends to be the deciding criterion if your words are contradictory.

5. Is one of the most obvious differences between people with power and those with little or no power.

INTRODUCTIONS

When people meet, introductions follow. Introductions are an everyday custom in the business world. Knowing how to introduce others properly, who to introduce to whom in order to show respect, and when to introduce yourself, are all part of the social skills involved with meeting others.

Introductions are necessary because people tend to feel awkward talking to people they do not know. Introductions can pave the way for creating interest, lessening hesitation or embarrassment, making way for engaging conversation, and helping generate a desire for furthering the acquaintance. Etiquette and good manners dictate that we always make introductions even if the individuals may be previously acquainted.

The following are the scenarios you often encounter:

■ Introducing two people to each other

■ Introducing more than two people

■ Introducing one person to a larger group of people

■ Introducing oneself to others

Let's look at each of these situations.

Basic Introductions

Introduction basics are used whether at a formal event or a ball game. When you are introducing two people, always introduce *each* person to the other. Although some etiquette experts consider this practice repetitious, it makes sense, out of respect, to honor each person in the introduction. For example, suppose your are at a ball game with Bill, and you run into your friend Jan. A quick introduction would sound like this:

> "Jan, this is Bill, an army buddy. Bill this is Jan. She works in the same building."

Also correct is the following:

> "Jan, Bill; Bill, Jan."

The advantage of repeating both names is to give everyone a chance to hear each name twice, thus making it easier to remember names.

Keep your introductions simple when you are first practicing how to do them smoothly. As you go along, you will learn how to gracefully add more information about each person as you introduce them. For example, the following is a very simple introduction.

> "Mr. Kembel, may I introduce Jack Novak. Jack, this is Ralph Kembel."

If you add more information, the introduction might become the following:

> "Mr. Kembel, may I introduce a good friend, Jack Novak. Jack, this is Ralph Kembel, an outstanding events coordinator. I was the keynote speaker at an incentive meeting he planned."

Keep the following in mind to guide you in showing respect by who you introduce to whom.

- Introduce an associate *to* a client or guest.
- Introduce a younger person *to* an older person.
- Introduce a lower ranking person *to* an upper ranking person.
- Introduce an untitled person *to* a titled person.
- Introduce a young woman *to* an older man.
- Introduce a young man *to* a young woman.
- Introduce younger couples *to* older couples.

An easy way to always mention people in the correct order is to look at the person who deserves the greatest honor, and state that person's name first.

> "Grandpa, I'd like you to meet a good friend, Char Kennedy. Char, this is my grandfather, Mr. Olsen."

Business Introductions

Although making introductions is a very important business skill, few people know how to do it properly. The following lists give you the most important points to remember about the kind of introduction.

■ When making business introductions, remember the following four important points.
1. Introduce *both* people to each other.
2. Use *both* first and last names.
3. Introduce the person with lesser rank, status, position, or age *to* the other.
4. Make eye contact with each person.

■ Introduce a client to an associate as follows.

> "Sharon Carpenter, this is my new associate, Joyce Caplin. Joyce, this is Sharon Carpenter, the director of personnel for Aubrey & Associates, a long-time client."

> "Steve Mason, this is our department manager, Gus Harris. Gus Harris, this is Steve Mason, one of our biggest customers."

■ Introduce a student to a manager as follows.

> "Steve Baker, may I introduce Heidi Andersen, one of the top accounting students from the University of North Dakota. Heidi, this is Steve Baker, one of our managers."

■ Introduce a partner or officer of the company to a new employee as follows.

> "Ms. Bennett, may I introduce our new payroll manager, Steve Case. Steve this is Joanne Bennett, one of our partners."

■ Introduce equals at a function or event as follows.

> "Kay, this is Carol Olson, owner of Prestige Personnel. Carol, this is Kay Miller, who is a partner in the firm of Miller & Kelly."

■ Introduce a person to several others as follows.

1. If there are two other people with you when you introduce the third, follow the same format as when introducing two people.

   "George, Steve, I'd like you to meet a new member, Jim Benson. Jim, this is George Waters and Steve Mailer."

2. If there are more than two others, following this format creates a jumble. In this case you would say the following.

   "Jim, I'd like to introduce you to several of our members. [*Then go around the group in order*]. George Waters, Steve Mailer, Sandy Winston, Henriette Klein, and Dan Mueller. This is Jim Benson, a new member."

3. In larger groups, introduce the person to a few people close by and then it is up to that person to introduce him- or herself to others present.

If you have clients touring your office and you take them through several of the departments, you may want to introduce them to the head of each department, or the person that would be handling their account in some manner. Handshakes would not be expected to follow; an acknowledging nod and a "hello" is appropriate.

Responding to Introductions

When responding to an introduction, look at the person you're being introduced to, offer your hand, and say the following.

"It's nice to meet you, Mr. Olsen."

Other acceptable responses include the following.

"How do you do, Ms. Bass."

"I'm glad to meet you, Mr. Novak."

Avoid unacceptable replies such as the following.

"Pleazed ta meet cha."

Good grammar and pronunciation are always the goal in business. These are too youthful and casual.

"Hi!"

"Howdy!"

This is too formal, icy, and stiff. ·

"I'm pleased to make your acquaintance."

There is a lot of confusion over the proper time to use a person's first name at the initial introduction. The following are some guidelines.

■ If the person is closer to your parents' ages than yours, use the last name.

■ If the person is higher ranking than you in a profession or organization, using the last name is a better choice.

■ If the person is a new customer or client, use their last name.

■ If the person is from another country, *always* use their last name.

■ If the person is about the same age or rank, first names can be used.

When in doubt, err on the side of formality. It shows respect for the other person, and at that point, you will be asked to use the other person's first name if that is what he or she prefers. You do not want to make a negative impression by appearing too casual or disrespectful.

Self-Introductions

How many times has someone come up to you, started talking, and you did not know who he or she was? A self-introduction would have been appropriate. An effective personal introduction would give people your name, what you do or who you work for, and a comment that adds interest. It might sound like one of the following.

"Hello. May I join you? My name is Randi Freidig and I'm a new Chamber member."

"Hello, I haven't had a chance to meet you. I'm Scott Conahan and an active member in the state society."

A friend and colleague, Vanna Novak, who specializes in communication skills, suggests the following format if you are asked to introduce yourself before any professional group. She calls these "*introductions that sell.*"[17]

1. Start by getting the attention of the group. An energetic "Good morning!" with a warm smile would work.

2. Next, move immediately into saying something that will generate interest or curiosity around what you do.

---

[17] Vanna Novak, M.C. Communications, Seattle, WA.

3. Now, say what it is you do.

4   State the name of your company.

5. State your name. (Notice that this is one of the last things you mention.)

6. Close by saying something that indicates your genuine interest in the group.

Do not leave your self-introduction to chance. It will create interest and can enhance your credibility. Examples are the following.

> "Good morning! I work for the company that makes the little black boxes in airplanes, XXX Company. I'm the Vice President of Finance. My name is Betsy Moeller and I'm looking forward to getting involved with you and this very worthwhile project."

> "Hello! I'm the one at Larson & Associates who is responsible for getting all the computers to work together. I'm a CPA and my name is Bruce Jones. It's a real pleasure to have the opportunity to get involved in the Small Business Council."

Introductions Do's and Don'ts

There are a number of do's and don'ts to keep in mind that will help you develop a smooth, gracious approach to introductions. The following are good practices.

■ Do remember that business introductions are based on rank and hierarchy, not gender. Social etiquette is based on chivalry, which dictates that introductions, both formal and informal, are made according to age, then gender, then social status. In business etiquette, however, hierarchy, rank, and status come first.

■ Do address women as "Ms.," which is accepted today. If you are addressing an older woman whom you know to be married and who prefers "Mrs.," do respect her preference.

■ Do respond to introductions by extending your hand and looking at the person to whom you are being introduced.

There are a number of things that should be avoided as well. Consider the following.

■ Don't use an honorific when introducing yourself, which will come across as pretentious. For example, don't say the following.

> "My name is Ms. Freidig."

■ Don't make an issue out of anything that might embarrass another person. For example, if a person is introducing you to someone you already know, let them do so.

■ Don't let your tone or wording come across in the wrong context. Avoid making introductions like the following that come across as demanding.

> "You remember me, don't you?" (Just introduce yourself!)

> "Dale, you remember the Randoys, don't you?" (This puts Dale on the spot.)

> "Jim, meet my cousin, Evan." (This is too demanding.)

> "Dr. Levy, shake hands with my partner, Suzanne Olsen." (This sounds like an order.)

GETTING THE NAMES RIGHT

One of the most important words you can ever use is a person's name. Mispronouncing or using the wrong name is a sure way to show your ignorance and lack of consideration. If you are introduced to a Michael or a Debra, do not say, "Hello, Mike" or "Hi, Debbie." To do so shows you were not listening, or simply do not care. Nicknames or shortened versions of names are considered friendly in some places and by some people. Do not, however, make assumptions. Your fondness for shortened names may not be shared by the person whose name you are changing.

The following are important considerations to keep in mind during introductions:

■ Always make a point of standing when being introduced.

■ If you forget someone's name as you are about to introduce them, the important thing is to acknowledge it quickly and graciously so the introduction can proceed. Turn to that person and say something like one of the following.

> "Please help me out. Your name just slipped my mind."

> "It's been one of those days. Please remind me of your name."

■ If you have not been introduced, offer your name as soon as possible.

■ If you are approached by someone who's name has slipped your mind, offer yours immediately.

■ If you did not catch the person's name, ask immediately. For example, you might say the following.

> "I'm sorry, I didn't catch your name."

■ If you are unsure of the pronunciation of a person's name, ask. People with unusual names appreciate this.

■ If someone addresses you by the wrong name, correct it immediately. Others will appreciate knowing how to address you correctly. You might say one of the following.

> "Oh, my name is Randi, not Sandy, a common mistake!"

> "I go by Katherine rather than Kathy."

■ If someone's name tag reads "Steven" and you were just introduced to him as "Steve," ask which he prefers, and make note of it.

■ If someone asks which name you prefer, "Steven" or "Steve," pick one, even though you really do not have a preference. It puts the other person at ease about your name.

■ If you are wearing gloves at a formal event or outside because it is very cold, you need not remove them for handshakes.

Make a habit of offering your name along with a handshake in order to spare others the embarrassment of having to ask. Bear in mind that even people who have met you before may have trouble recollecting who you are if you have crossed paths in a different context.

REMEMBERING NAMES

Forgetting names is a common dilemma. Developing memory skills will help you recollect names. Repetition is the way to improve this skill, and I have found that association techniques are helpful. For example, while I was watching television, I realized how often I forget names. I noticed I could never remember the names of local television news anchors. In our area, there has been a high turnover of these newscasters, and I used that fact as an opportunity to practice memory skills.

One of our news anchors is Teresa Green. I pictured her with "tears" of paper—torn green paper—coming out of her head, her ears, her nose, and her mouth. The more bizarre the association, the more senses tend to be involved, and the higher the likelihood of remembering the name. The word *tear*, like in tearing paper, sounds similar to Teresa. *Tear*, as in the liquid that flows from your eyes when sad, would also work.

The skill to master is getting to the association fast. Sitting in my family room watching television news gives me plenty of time to think. When meeting someone at a Chamber of Commerce event, however, I need to be quick. So practice every chance you get.

The following will help you develop the skill.

■ Repeat a new name to yourself as soon as you hear it.

■ Use it in your greeting. For example, you might say the following.

"It's so nice to meet you, Ms. Green."

■ Make a point to use the name at least once more while speaking to the person. Do not overuse it.

■ Develop association techniques by studying books, listening to audio tapes, or taking memory development classes.

SHAKING HANDS

A discussion on meeting and greeting people would not be complete without addressing the handshake. Americans shake hands less than people from any other part of the world. Perhaps that explains the surprisingly poor and unimpressive handshakes of so many people. Handshakes are often too firm, too limp, or just awkward. Worst of all, some people only offer their fingers!

Nevertheless, your handshake deserves careful attention because it is an important part of the first impression that you make on others. It is also a parting gesture that helps you gracefully conclude any number of conversations or other events.

It is appropriate to shake hands in any of the following situations.

■ You are first introduced to someone.

■ You take leave of a person you have just met, saying goodbye.

■ You enter a room, greeting people you know and being introduced to others.

■ Someone comes into your office from outside the company.

■ Someone comes into your office from within the company but whom you do not see often.

■ You run into someone outside your office.

In the predominant culture in the United States, a good handshake consists of the following.

■ Hands connect at the webbed part of the thumb.

■ Fingers wrap around the back of the hand.

■ The wrist is held straight, not broken or bent.

■ A medium-to-firm grip displays confidence without being bone-crushing.

■ Two to three pumps last about two to three seconds.

The following make a handshake less than impressive:

- Offering the back of the hand to the person, with the wrist bent and the fingers usually pointing toward the floor
- Breaking at the knuckles, which gives a "pincher" effect and is more of a finger shake than a handshake
- Weak or fish-limp shakes
- Bone-crushing shakes
- Pumping or hanging on forever
- Patting the back of the other person's hand with your left hand, which is considered condescending
- Touching and patting

Special Considerations

- If you tend to have clammy hands, carry a handkerchief or quickly brush the palm of your hand over your slacks or skirt.
- At events, hold your drink in your left hand, so you do not have to switch hands and offer a cold, wet hand for the shake.
- Socially, a gentleman would wait for the lady to offer her hand to initiate the handshake. Business manners, however, put women on equal footing, so the handshake can be initiated by either gender. The point is to shake hands.
- If you have offered your hand, and the other person's hand does not come out to meet it, simply drop yours, or use it as a gesture to enhance your words. For example, you might turn your hand palm up while saying, "It's nice to meet you."
- Someone with an injured right hand or no right hand at all may offer his or her left hand. Simply rotate your right wrist and grasp the extended hand, or offer your left hand.
- When meeting someone in a wheelchair who does not or cannot offer his or her hand, lightly touch the person's arm above the wrist and indicate your pleasure at meeting him or her.
- If you have arthritic hands, and do not offer them for handshakes, be sure you sound and look enthused to meet the person. You can also make a comment such as the following. "I'm so pleased to meet you. Please pardon my arthritic hands. They don't respond well to handshakes."

If it is someone else whose hands are arthritic, be understanding. Some people prefer not to draw attention to their affliction.

142

Be Easy to Meet

The following are hints on how to be approachable and visible.

- If you are wearing a name tag, place it on the upper right side, the side closest to anyone with whom you are shaking hands.
- If you prepare your own name tag, make sure you write your name in large, legible block letters.
- If the name tag has been prepared for you and your name is incorrect, correct it.
- Keep your right arm and hand free, in order to easily offer it for the handshake.
- Be prepared to give a self-introduction.
- Offer your name often.

Since a critical part of your marketing strategy is to meet people, you will want to feel confident and comfortable doing so. You want people's experience with you to be positive, and everyone responds favorably to courteous, well-mannered behavior.

■ ■ ■

Keep the following in mind when meeting and greeting people.

- Making a good first impression is worth the effort.
- A person's perceived credibility is closely linked to nonverbal behaviors.
- Dress appropriately to show your self-respect and respect for others.
- Dress according to the occasion, the environment, and the message you want to send.
- Be aware of the message your nonverbal behaviors send.
- If there is a conflict between the verbal and nonverbal messages you send, people believe the nonverbal.
- Circulate and introduce yourself at any function, large or small, especially if the host(s) are busy.
- Both women and men should always stand for introductions and shaking hands.
- If someone mispronounces your name during the introduction, make the correction in a positive manner.
- If you did not hear the other person's name, ask.
- Since a person's name is representative of their identity, do not mispronounce or shorten the name, nor make jokes or disparaging remarks about it.

143

- If you have a difficult name to pronounce, assist the person trying to pronounce it by stating it slowly or offering a word that "sounds like" it.

- Always make introductions, even if you cannot remember a name.

- If you have forgotten a name, simply ask that person for his or her name, and continue the introduction. For example, look at the person whose name you have forgotten and say, "Please help me out, I've forgotten your name."

- Never use "Mr." or "Mrs." when referring to your own spouse.

- Always provide your spouse's last name if it is different from yours.

Chapter 11

THE VALUE
OF VISIBILITY

*"Forget about market surveys
and analyst reports. Word of
mouth is probably the most
powerful form of communication
in the business world."*

—*Regis McKenna, author*

Creating visibility for your firm and yourself is an ongoing process requiring persistence and patience. You want people to know about you and how to reach you. Ideally, you want and need to keep your name and the name of your firm out in the community all the time. Turning every contact into a marketing opportunity takes planning. And, with time and experience, you will become more sophisticated and selective about your activities.

Name familiarity opens doors. In this chapter, we will look at various ways you can create visibility for both you and your firm. Your marketing and public relations efforts should not stop during tax season. On the contrary, this can be the most rewarding time to step up marketing efforts because it is the time everyone is focused on tax planning, which leads to the other services you provide.

SPEAK OUT!

Public speaking takes many forms. Whether you are presenting a proposal to a potential client, leading a meeting, or conducting a seminar, your ability to persuade, educate, and inform all depends on your public speaking skills.

There is no better way to build these skills than to join a Toastmasters Club. Toastmasters International has clubs throughout the world. Some meet weekly, some biweekly. Some meet at breakfast, some at lunch, and others after work. Toastmasters provides a good environment in which to learn how to be a better public speaker and presenter, to think on your feet, to organize thoughts for the best impact, to distinguish between persuading and informing. And it builds confidence.

I joined a Toastmasters Club years ago, even though I had been training and speaking for years. One member, at that time, mentioned he got involved with Toastmasters because he observed that the men at the top in his company were all good public speakers. It was definitely a skill needed for advancement within his organization and industry. Another member, a CPA with a speech impediment, became one of our most accomplished and eloquent speakers.

Your ability to articulate and clearly communicate ideas, make technical information understandable and relevant, and present yourself as a good communicator gives you an edge. Good public speaking skills will distinguish you from your competitors.

One of the most important things to remember about speaking is how your audience learns. Some people are predominantly auditory in their learning styles. Others are more visual. Some are kinesthetic. A good public speaker reaches each of these groups by the way the material is written and presented. Consider the following about what we learn.

- 75 percent comes to us visually.
- 13 percent comes through hearing.
- 12 percent comes from smell, taste, and touch.

Although most of all public speaking informs others, its most powerful use is to persuade someone to action. The latter is your purpose when you are presenting proposals to potential or existing clients. You want them to hire you or add more services.

Dave Peoples, in his book *Presentations Plus*, reveals some information that is critical to being successful when making presentations.[18] When visual aids are used, people are more likely to be persuaded to the course of action you want them to take. A pictorial representation of a point you are making will increase retention and comprehension by six times. If you only show the picture and say nothing, the comprehension and retention will be three and one-half times greater than if you just say the words. A study at the Wharton School of the University of Pennsylvania concluded that the use of visual aids (in this case, overhead transparencies) has the following effects.

- People are more likely to say "yes" and act on your recommendation.
- You will be perceived as being more professional, persuasive, credible, interesting, and better prepared.
- The probability of the audience reaching a consensus is 79 percent versus 58 percent without visual aids.

Another study done at the University of Minnesota came to similar conclusions along with the startling revelation that people are 43 percent more likely to be persuaded if you use visual aids.

Visual aids take on a whole new look now with the availability of computer-generated visuals, but do not get carried away. You are still the one that must connect with the audience and influence how they *perceive* you. You want them to trust you, believe you, listen to you, respect you, and to move toward a course of action that reflects your agenda.

Let's examine how these skills can be used to create visibility for you and your business.

---

[18] David A. Peoples. *Presentations Plus*. New York: John Wiley & Sons, 1988.

Classes and Seminars

Knowledge is power and yet we all seem to be overwhelmed by what we need to know, what we want to know, and how best to learn. If you can assimilate and present information in an organized and interesting way, teaching classes and leading seminars is a great way to showcase your skills and talents as well as bring in business. Look around in your community for opportunities to teach, including the following:

- College and university classes
- General seminars open to the public
- Informational seminars for clients and referral sources
- State society or association for CPAs, which conducts CPE classes, chapter meetings, and conferences
- Chapter meetings for special interest groups

Do not expect to generate a major income stream from these classes and seminars. You will be compensated either at an hourly rate for actual class time, a flat fee, or not at all. Consider your time as part of your marketing investment. Community colleges and universities with extension programs are always looking for experts to share information with their students. Contact the business department to explore ideas and subjects that would complement the current curriculum.

Seminars and classes open to the public work best if they are sponsored, usually by a trade or professional association, or by your firm and other professional service providers. When sponsored, the mailing list, direct mail pieces, and publicity are more targeted and effective at bringing in attendees. Richard Dance, a highly regarded CPA in Seattle, built a solid following from workshops he presented for the annual conferences for Women In Business.

An example of a cosponsored seminar might be on the topic of succession planning for closely held companies. Your firm might team up with a law firm you routinely work with. Another topic might focus on how small businesses can get a loan. Here, your firm would team up with a bank you and your clients do business with.

These topics and many others would also interest your current clients. By designing an informational seminar for your clients and referral sources, you add value to the relationships.

Your state CPA society or association is another good place to offer your expertise in the form of a workshop. Call the person in charge of continuing professional education to explore ideas.

Every city and town has local chapters of special interest groups—trade, professional, or civic—that are listed in your local telephone book under "Associations." Most have annual meetings or conferences that require speakers. Jaycees offer seminars to their members. Bankers attend conferences specific to their needs. Call to find out who is in charge of programs and conferences, targeting those associations that fit into your marketing plan. Local papers usually list upcoming seminars and workshops, including the speaker's name. (Eventually, it will be yours!)

Speaking Opportunities

As a professional speaker, I know there are many opportunities to speak both for a fee or honorarium or for free. Trade and professional associations are always looking for knowledgeable, effective presenters who can offer valuable insight into new legislation, accounting systems for small businesses, reading financial statements, effective financing strategies, tax and financial planning, and a myriad of other subjects that will help members be better at what they do.

Any time you can speak in front of a group, you have the chance to practice your speaking techniques, develop ideas, build stories and anecdotes, develop and use visuals, and build your confidence. Explore your community for the many opportunities to speak. It is a great way to sell yourself, your firm, and your services.

Service organizations, such as the Rotary and Kiwanis, usually meet weekly and are always looking for speakers. They give the speakers from ten to thirty minutes. This is a wonderful training ground for those who are serious about developing their speaking skills and topics.

Every city has dozens of organizations and associations that meet less frequently, usually monthly. A timely topic presented to business owners or mortgage bankers at their monthly association meeting positions you as a valuable resource. Industry association meetings are another good opportunity to gain visibility within an area of special interest.

Often, you will need to make the first contact. Do some research on the organizations you have targeted. Get to know the kinds of topics that have been presented in the past. Have a few topic suggestions in mind when you make that first call. Also, check with your state society to see if they have a speaker's bureau.

Another occasion to speak will come if you volunteer to head up committees within the community. This might be at your church, Jaycees, the state CPA society, community citizens group, or as a volunteer with the United Way. Do not make light of these opportunities to speak; do all you can to prepare.

Many CPAs use public speaking as a way to promote their business or expertise. It gives people a chance to observe you, hear what you have to say and how you say it, and they can evaluate you before going to the expense of hiring you. It helps get your foot in the door! And do not forget to bring a handout that highlights your key points and tells the participants how to reach you.

THE MIGHTY PEN

Roger Bel Air, a friend of mine, has written several books, one of which is about working with bankers. We have had many discussions about the value of writing a book versus writing articles to create visibility. His opinion is that articles can be a much more effective way of getting visibility and building a reputation. There are ten thousand copies in print of his book, *How to Borrow Money from a Banker*.[19] One article he wrote on working with bankers that appeared in *Success Magazine* reached 350,000 people. His exposure from that article was much greater than that he gained from the book. Another advantage to writing articles for national, trade and industry magazines, and association publications is that you have the credibility of the organization behind you.

The point? Start small and target local or regional publications. Unless you have a book in you, start with short articles. Writing is a wonderful way to clarify the key points you frequently make with clients and associates. Since you work with people to help them make better business and financial decisions, you can address many topics that would be of interest to the community at large.

There are many vehicles for articles. The most obvious are your community papers and business journals. Another is trade and industry publications. For instance, ask to write an article for the monthly newsletter of the Associated General Contractors. Make sure the topic appeals to the business and industry. This is a great way to be viewed as a resource.

Magazines

It is more difficult to publish in national magazines. You might want to consider getting the help of a publicist if you are trying to get articles placed in national publications. However, trade, industry, and other regional business magazines are much more receptive. In the library, you can find publication sources such as *Writer's Market* and *The Magazine Industry Marketplace*, which tell you about the circulation, whether or not the magazine accepts articles, the length of the standard article, how often the magazine is published, and who to contact. Look up an industry you are active in. You will be absolutely amazed at how many magazines are published within that industry. Each has a target audience and it may not be the same as yours.

---

[19] Roger Bel Air. *How to Borrow Money from a Banker*. New York: AMACOM, 1988.

Many associations put out magazines or other monthly publications as a service and benefit to their members. These may be perfect vehicles for your articles and will help create the visibility you want within an industry.

Newspapers

Become visible as an expert by writing a column for your local community newspaper. It may be on the importance of succession planning or how cash flow can influence small businesses. Many of the dailies also are interested in experts who can write concise articles to educate their readers. Most larger communities have a weekly business journal.

Before you approach a newspaper about a column, do your homework. What are the demographics of the readership? How long are the average columns? Is there a strong business community involved? What is the tone of the editors? What kind of topics can be tied to frequent articles? Notice any trends? Study how the articles are written—who, what, where, when, why, and how?

Letters to the Editor

Do not laugh off the opportunity of letters to the editor. This is an effective way to get exposure too. Every trade publication, business journal, and local daily has a "Letters" section. It's a way to express your opinion, point out a solution, bring to light a problem or trend, or simply to acknowledge another writer or leader in the industry or community. Any time you read the business journal or a trade publication, look at the articles and the actions of the people mentioned. Find a way to comment on the subject of one of the articles, or to acknowledge the accomplishments of a businessperson highlighted in an article. You would be surprised by how many people read these letters.

Newsletters

Whether it is a firm newsletter or a nationally circulated newsletter, the opportunity is the same: to showcase your knowledge and expertise. Think about all the national newsletters or special reports you could subscribe to as a CPA. Every other profession has newsletters available to them as well. Each time I have had an article in *The Practicing CPA* or the *CPA Marketing Report*, I get calls and requests for more information.

At the local level, a newsletter put out by your firm for clients is a marketing tool that many CPAs have found to be very effective. Articles need to be relevant, short, educational, and graphically attractive. There are many variations, costs, and inescapable frustrations involved with producing a newsletter. As with any marketing tool, the effect is cumulative. And do not forget to put key media contacts on your mailing list.

Chris McDevitt, a local practitioner in Edmonds, a town north of Seattle, gave me a copy of a newsletter he puts out in cooperation with three other independent professionals in the community. They all specialize in and understand the business and professional needs of physicians and health care providers. The newsletter is titled *The Edmonds Doctor*. Each of the four professionals—a CPA, a lawyer, an insurance broker, and a banker—has a full page. Their objective is to position themselves as experts in a specific industry to which they provide advice, products, and services.

Special Reports

Another effective way to disseminate information on a specific topic is to write a special report. It looks like an article that might have appeared in a magazine, but has never been formally published. The focus can be a new law or regulation that impacts a specific industry or group of clients. Or it might be a more general topic of interest. The end result is a mailing that gives you the opportunity to stay in touch with clients and community resources by providing them something of value.

Press Releases

Never pass up an opportunity to announce a promotion, a seminar, an award, or any other activity that can be sent to the media. A public relations consultant or firm can be extremely valuable in this area. Whenever your firm has something newsworthy, put it in the form of a press release. This would include the following:

- Promotions or the addition of partners
- Merging with another firm
- Awards received or other kinds of community recognition
- Announcing new offices or a move to a new location
- Expansion of services
- Making a forecast or reporting on a trend
- Comments on new legislation and regulations

Press releases should be timely and newsworthy. There is a specific format for news releases, so you will want to have that available to you.

The Marketing Advantage, a book put out by the AICPA Management of an Accounting Practice Committee, goes more deeply into the details of the mechanics of creating visibility. It is a great reference to have on your library shelves.

Remember, if you speak or write on any subject, you want to keep your target market in mind. For example, if you are developing an expertise and reputation within the hospitality industry, you want exposure to the movers and shakers and decision makers within that industry. Ideally, it would be nice to be featured at an industry conference or in a trade magazine. However, influentials also read other business publications, attend meetings outside their industry, and are involved in their communities. Most of the time, the path to these leaders is not direct. Have patience.

BE QUOTABLE

Being a resource to the media can be both planned and spontaneous. Many times your name appears on a media list of experts because you are a published author or you have been quoted by other media sources. Relations with the media need to be a two-way street. Be accessible when they call. In fact, drop everything in order to be available. And, every now and then, call them with a story idea or new twist to a subject of interest. Stay alert to public relations opportunities.

If part of your marketing plan is to position yourself as an expert, remember to let the media know. Your extensive training and experience as an accountant give you insight into a variety of business topics, including taxation, Securities and Exchange Commission compliance, coping with new accounting standards, cash flow, industry trends, and the general economic climate for business growth. Having the knowledge and facts to be considered an expert by the media, though, also must include the ability to be a clear, concise, and interesting communicator.

Depending on the size of your firm and the nature of your local media, your efforts here need to be tailored to your budget, time, and resources. Positive media relations will help your firm with its image and reputation. It helps create visibility and awareness. And through the media you can get public recognition for superior achievements and leadership in accounting.

Working with the media requires certain skills, so do your homework or hire a public relations expert. Find out what kind of stories they consider newsworthy; how journalists work; the best way to get the firm's message out; how to handle print, radio, and television interviews; how to control a crisis or bad press.

Having positive media relations is very rewarding and goes a long way toward creating visibility in your community and industry.

VOLUNTEER

Public service can be rewarding personally and professionally. It gives you the opportunity to give back to your community by volunteering your time and talents. At the same time, you and your firm get noticed for doing so. Another objective is also met when goodwill is eventually converted to business.

Since there are many organizations you could serve, it is important to keep the following in mind when choosing.

- Does it interest you?
- Can you develop new skills in the position?
- Will it allow you to use your professional skills?
- Who else is involved? Who are the members?
- Does it offer the potential for visibility?
- Will you feel like you can make a difference?
- Is there room for advancement to other positions with greater responsibility and exposure?
- What kind of time commitment is involved?

If you are just beginning your career, some obvious opportunities may be found among your family and leisure activities. Coach a Little League team, run for a position on the school board or PTA, get involved with day care organizations, or volunteer at church.

A wide variety of organizations provide the chance to grow with other professionals. Jaycees and the Junior League are good examples. You will find that the other members are also growing in their careers. A few years down the road, you will be able to refer business to each other and share key information and resources.

Volunteer for a hospital committee, serve on the board of your local Boys and Girls Club, get involved in the arts. Don Luby, a local practitioner, volunteered to help with a dance marathon that benefitted the Special Olympics. Now, years later, he is the chairman of his state's board for the Special Olympics. His involvement with this organization has given him personal satisfaction, as well as many clients through the contacts he made.

Many CPAs and their firms strategically target certain causes and organizations with which they want to be involved and associated. Decisions are often influenced by which nonprofit clients, referral sources, and key community leaders are involved. A number of organizations get extensive, valuable media coverage. Sponsoring an event that benefits a specific organization can be very rewarding.

Two CPAs played in a golf tournament that benefited a local hospital's center that provides help to children who have been sexually assaulted. The CPAs got so hooked on the cause that they volunteered to chair the following year's tournament. Then, they persuaded their accounting firm to become a lead sponsor for the tournament and to host firm members, clients, and key resources. Rather than host their own golf tournament, the firm decided to support this good cause by giving their clients a day of golf. That year, eighty-four clients, contacts, and partners participated in the tournament. An additional ten clients who do not play golf came to the banquet to show their support—definitely a win-win situation for everyone involved.

Although your eye is on building alliances, meeting key civic personalities, and gaining visibility, the bigger objective is business development. I can offer this caution, however: Do not sign up or volunteer if you can't follow through. There is nothing more frustrating than a committee or board member who says that he or she will do something and then never does. Letting people down will only damage your personal reputation and the image of the firm.

Volunteering is a rewarding way to practice and develop your personal marketing skills, build credibility, and enhance your attitude toward giving back to the world at large.

■ ■ ■

Keep the following in mind when seeking visibility.

- Visibility helps create name familiarity. You want people to think of you first.
- Learn to recognize opportunities to get visibility.
- Writing articles for well-placed magazines and newsletters will often reach more people than a writing a book.
- Look for opportunities to teach classes in the community and through your state CPA organization.
- Never pass up an opportunity to speak before a group.
- Always be well prepared before you speak to a group or teach a class.
- Be realistic. Do not overcommit to more than you can actually do.
- Make sure your marketing and public relations efforts are targeted to the right market.
- Effective public relations is a cumulative process, not an event.
- Volunteer to help worthy causes.
- Stay in touch with the people you meet through your outside activities.

SETTING YOURSELF APART FROM THE COMPETITION

"Differences between peak performers and their less productive coworkers are much smaller than most people think . . . extraordinary achievers are ordinary people who have found ways to make a major impact."

—*Charles Garfield, author*

"The trouble with the rat race is that even if you win you're still a rat."

—*Lily Tomlin, actress and comic*

DO LOTS OF LITTLE THINGS

Superior performers learned long ago that it is more effective to be one percent better at hundreds of things, rather than 100 percent better at one or two things. Surprise your clients by doing many little things of higher value—go beyond what is expected.

One CPA who has a keen interest in cars helps clients buy new automobiles. He found that his clients were uncomfortable or unskilled at negotiating a good deal—exactly what he relishes. Another firm offers pickup and delivery for individual tax returns. An E-mail address gives one firm's clients timely access to expertise, advice, and help on business subjects. Reminder cards, checklists, educational tools, and an abundance of other small personal touches help distinguish you from the competition.

Clients who get added value from their CPAs typically are more willing to pay higher professional fees and to make referrals for accounting services. The following are some ideas.

- People remember little courtesies and small kindnesses.
- When leaving a voice or E-mail, always include your full name and phone number.
- Include a small surprise when clients pick up their tax returns (for instance, an individual packet of aspirin, with a clever note, or a candy bar to sweeten the news).
- Be sure your client knows how to get in contact with you any time during stressful periods.
- Follow through on all client inquires, requests, and complaints.
- Return all client calls within an hour or two.
- Call just to see how they are doing.
- Refer business to your clients.
- Help your clients expand their resources through alliances with other businesses.
- Do business with your clients' businesses—buy from your clients.
- Acknowledge your client's special occasions.
- Help negotiate the purchase or lease of a new car for your clients.
- When a client needs experts in other fields, help locate them by maintaining a database of outside experts.
- Be able to recommend bankers who are happy to serve small business owners and self-employed professionals.
- Act as a talent scout when your clients need key personnel.

- Send articles or tip sheets, with notes explaining how the information might concern their business.
- Do more than sign your holiday cards. Add personal notes letting your clients know how important they are to you and your business. (Start months in advance!)
- Go out of your way to thank your clients and referral sources.
- Send a thank-you note to all your 1040 clients within a few days of delivery of the return.

BE SENSITIVE AND ATTENTIVE TO YOUR CLIENTS' NEEDS

Rather than just performing duties, work to obtain results. See yourself as your client's partner—someone who is also very interested in seeing the client's business grow and prosper. See each and every problem or obstacle, no matter how small, as an opportunity to build the relationship with the client. For instance, take time to explain the findings of an audit or financial report. Make sure your client understands the implications. Consider the following.

- Be honest about mistakes and try to build togetherness in solving them.
- Let your client take credit for the outcome of the project.
- Ask questions that will let your clients know you want to understand their issues better.
- Recognize formal client hierarchies.
- Understand key decision makers and the power and politics of the organization.
- Let them know you are available any time they need to discuss an issue.

BE WILLING TO ASK HOW YOU ARE DOING

You and your client may or may not have the same perspective of the quality of your work. When asked what partners thought clients wanted, the top three answers were not the same as the client's answers to the question, "What do you most want from your CPA?" It is much better to know earlier in the engagement rather than later. It is an important process to think through—how and when to get feedback on the quality of your people and your services. Research has shown that an unsatisfied client who is acknowledged and has satisfactory resolve becomes a more loyal client. The following are possible steps.

1. Start by asking, "What do you care about?" to identify client interests, perceptions, and values.

2. Find ways to uncover your client's expectations.

3. Use client satisfaction surveys and other instruments to discover others' perceptions of your firm and the services you offer.

4. Use this information to assess new services and new opportunities.

5. Feedback from clients will help highlight and profess your firm's strengths.

6. Design ways to communicate these strengths and the quality of your service to clients and prospects.

7. Failure to follow through with client comments and suggestions can have a negative effect on the firm's image.

8. Do not hesitate to ask your client for input when you are face-to-face.

9. Organize informal roundtable discussions with key clients to solicit feedback on how to better serve them.

BE AN ADVOCATE FOR CLIENT DEVELOPMENT

It is important to see that building client relationships is the key to future work. Become an advocate of your clients. Emphasize maximizing the quality and value of existing client relationships. Maintain contact with clients when no specific project is under way. Preserve friendly contact even after a project is lost to a competitor. Remember the old adage, "No one cares how much you know until they know how much you care."

The following are specific steps you can take.

- Develop clients by sending articles, coaching and empowering them, and training.

- Identify and anticipate long-term problems and opportunities in the client system.

- Take the initiative to discover client needs and identify ways to meet those needs.

- Foster learning to help make your clients better consumers of your firm's services.

- Always put your client's needs over any others.

- Work to understand and appreciate different and opposing perspectives on an issue.

- Get actively involved in your clients' businesses.

- Do not wait for the client to call.

- Keep clients focused on their day-to-day operations.
- Devote part of every day to being with clients.
- Explore your client's thinking—you may not know how little you know about them.
- Always assume a need to know more.
- Become an active listener.
- Minimize mixed messages by monitoring communication.
- Improve your trustworthiness by improving your conduct—be predictable, clear, and honest, and take promises seriously.
- Conduct internal seminars for your most valued clients—prepared exclusively for them.
- Be an accessible business adviser to your clients.
- Find ways to help clients improve their profitability.

BE AN ADVOCATE FOR BUSINESS DEVELOPMENT

Without clients, there is no work. Without new clients, it is hard to grow and prosper. The relationship between client and business development and your future is clear. Clients offer you and your firm the opportunity to showcase and use your knowledge and expertise, to gain new experience, and to enjoy your livelihood. Every professional should be concerned with new business—where will that next engagement come from? This year? Next year? Being an advocate for developing a strong client and referral base is paramount to success for the CPA firm of the future.

- Seek the best ways to create visibility for you and your firm within your business community.
- Fine-tune your networking strategies.
- Enhance your people skills.
- Learn to ask for referrals from satisfied clients.
- Share your successes with others in the firm—help others build their business development skills.
- Understand the full range of services and expertise your firm offers in order to add value to current client services.
- Never leave business development opportunities to chance.
- Think of marketing expenditures as an investment, not an expense.
- Good research and consistent follow-through are vital to successful business development.
- Maintain relentless commitment to the marketing process.

ADOPT THE ENTREPRENEURIAL MIND-SET

The entrepreneurial mind is always asking questions. How can I (or we) do this better, faster? What will I (or we) need to know, which skills will be needed for my (or our) future success? Be willing to try new procedures, processes, implement new systems, and use creative brainstorming for problem solving. More of the same only brings more of the same. Consider the following.

- Investigate issues and known facts before making decisions.
- Use existing relationships to gain entry to the highest level in a target company.
- Constantly nurture existing professional relationships.
- Build new relationships in the context of future work-related goals.
- Take an active role in your career development.
- Continually ask whether the information you provide clients is in a format they can understand.
- See opportunity in all areas of your life.
- Keep your eyes open and your mind active.
- Develop your resourcefulness and use it.
- Be prepared.
- Have the courage to be creative, to think differently, to take a different approach.
- Seek understanding of differences before trying to solve them.
- Help build a management development library at your firm—people need to read about business matters, not just technical information.
- Look for new responsibilities.
- Continually build new skills.

The next five reminders focus more on the personal side. Much of the time we forget that others are observing us and making judgments about our ethics, values, and morals. Mark McCormack is an author and founder of a billion-dollar company, International Management Group. In his best-seller, *What They Don't Teach You At Harvard Business School*,[20] he cautions his readers to sharpen their awareness by observing people in business and social situations. He has found that people often reveal their innermost selves in the most innocent of situations. The less formal a situation or venue, the more likely people are to let

---

[20] Mark McCormack. *What They Don't Teach You at Harvard Business School.* New York: Bantam Books, 1984.

down their guards. He considers it very informative to watch how a person behaves toward a waiter or a reservationist, how they react to losing a point or a game on the tennis court, whether or not they take "gimmes" while putting, and how they handle a multitude of other situations. This kind of information helps him in his negotiations and contracts with sports clients and marketing customers.

Clients, associates, partners, and others you work with often appreciate the importance of business character and other inner qualities. You always want to exhibit your personal and professional best. The following sections spell out some reminders that are obvious to most.

NEVER EMBARRASS OTHERS

Do not undermine your trust in and respect of others. Learn to apologize sincerely when you embarrass someone or make a mistake. Remember, long after people have forgotten what you have said, they will remember how you made them feel. Keep the following in mind.

- Do not reprimand someone in front of others.
- Using another person as the butt of a joke is a mistake.
- Tell stories on yourself, not others.
- Graciously put up with others' poor manners.
- Ask first, before offering advice. Even better, wait until you are asked.
- When coaching or mentoring others, do so in private.
- Keep personal issues and events personal.
- Do not be the source of gossip.

BE EASY TO WORK WITH

Everyone, from receptionist to managing partner, should be easy to work with. Unfortunately, this is not the case. Distinguish yourself by focusing on what is important, not on personal feelings. Even if you find yourself working with someone you neither like nor respect, set aside your feelings. Try to give them what they need to do their job. Always be the consummate professional. Observe the following.

- Do not bring your sour or negative mood to work.
- Put things you borrow back where they belong.
- Keep your voice down to avoid interfering with the work of others.
- Learn to graciously give and accept compliments.
- Be a team player—do your part in a timely manner.
- Do not keep others waiting.

- Look for the positive in people and situations.
- Keep your work station or office clean, and clean up after yourself in public spaces.
- Say thanks to the staff and others within your company and your clients' companies.
- Remember the "one-minute compliment"—catch people doing something right.
- Treat everyone courteously and respectfully.
- Schedule time with others (managers, partners, clients), rather than "dropping by."
- Do not succumb to egotistical behavior as you gain fame, power, and fortune.
- Clarify what is expected of you and when it is expected.

WALK YOUR TALK

The power and simplicity of doing what you say you will do—walking your talk—benefits you as well as your relationship with the people around you. Practicing what you believe will help build a productive, enjoyable, and high-performance work environment. The following are some of the steps that will put you on the road to achieving the results you want.

- Adopt value-driven behaviors that lead to success in your business and personal life.
- Identify and eliminate "out-of-sync" behaviors that prevent you from reaching your goals.
- Use the power of your words and actions to build trust and credibility with coworkers and clients.
- Professing values and practicing them are two very different things.
- You earn the right to expect others to do things by first doing those things yourself.
- Practice what you preach—be a positive role model.

NEVER BURN BRIDGES

Solid interpersonal skills will build positive relationships. Think twice before you ever do anything to jeopardize an alliance with a client, an associate, a friend, or anyone else for that matter. You may never realize the amount of damage burning bridges (relationships) can do. One can lose business; be overlooked for a promotion, not recommended for an assignment, not invited to be part of a group, not welcomed on a team; and the list goes on. Always consider the following.

- Clear up any misunderstandings.
- If you have made a mistake, admit it and work to reverse it.
- When you have inadvertently offended someone, apologize.
- Send a note, flowers, candy, or some kind of peace offering when appropriate.
- Be accepting of others and their differing points of view.
- Avoid annoying habits such as bragging, insisting on one-upmanship, and coming across as a bigot.
- Do not seek free advice from those who charge for it.
- Do not give advice unless asked for it.
- Follow through on commitments.

BE THE BEST YOU CAN BE

Develop the habit of going the extra mile, which means providing more and better service than that for which you are paid, and do so with a positive mental attitude. Regularly ask yourself the following questions. Would I do business with me? Would I hire me? Would I promote me? Would I like working with me? Would I lay me off if we needed to reduce the number of professional staff?

- Show enthusiasm for your work, your coworkers, your firm, and your profession.
- Do a little more each day—take initiative.
- Activity will transform your dreams into reality and convert your ideas into actuality.
- Confront reality and move forward.
- Consider ideas without considering their practicality—expand options.
- Do not ignore the information superhighway. Take advantage of technological progress.
- Read biographies of successful people and successful companies—study their habits for success.
- Seek out quality people—those who share your vision and will support your growth.
- Be willing to share your gifts and talents.
- Dare to think big when setting goals, then plan smaller goals to help get you there.
- Do not do anything to embarrass yourself or your firm—on or off the job.
- Autograph your work with excellence.

Personal marketing skills revolve around your ability to build rapport with others and create visibility within your professional arena. These skills result in long-term positive business relationships that influence business development and career success. It is your ability to sell yourself and your talents to those who can make a difference. Developing that ability means making a commitment to forming personal marketing strategies, evaluating strengths and weaknesses, and improving relationship-building skills.

However, dreams and aspirations can only be achieved if you act upon the knowledge.

Dedicate yourself to excellence. Pursue your dreams and goals. Live up to your vision of your personal ideal. Take appropriate action. You can and will, then, achieve the confidence and polish necessary to succeed. Enjoy the process!

> *"If a man is called to be a streetsweeper, he should sweep streets even as Michelangelo painted or Beethoven composed music, or Shakespeare wrote poetry. He should sweep streets so well that all the hosts of heaven and earth will pause to say, here lived a great streetsweeper who did his job well."*
>
> — *Martin Luther King, Jr.*

APPENDIXES

APPENDIX A—SAMPLE WORKSHEET AND PERSONAL MARKETING PLAN

Part 1: Worksheet for Developing a Personal Marketing Plan

The purpose of this worksheet is to help the user develop a personal marketing plan that fits the current situation, helps the firm retain and grow its client base, and enhances career development. There are a number of questions that need to be answered and from those answers some goals and action should become obvious. The worksheet is best used if the individual is working with a coach or mentor.

Where are you now in your professional development? If your firm has position descriptions, which one best describes your current situation?

"I am a senior accountant responsible for preparing financial statements and tax returns. Occasionally, I review the work of staff accountants and our full-charge bookkeepers. I've been here four years and have my CPA certificate."

What could you be doing that would help those senior to you better serve existing clients?

"Learn which jobs are a priority with the partners. Hand down some of the easier, more routine work and ask for more challenging assignments."

Which industries do you really enjoy?

"The restaurant and manufacturing industries"

In which area of technical expertise do you want to become more proficient?

"Financial analysis and management"

How effective are you at:

Speaking in front of a group?	"Pretty good"
Conducting meetings?	"Don't know"
Listening?	"OK"
Writing?	"Very good"
Delegation?	"Not sure"
Consensus building?	"Haven't tried"

Selling or persuading?	"Don't do it"
Personally presenting a professional image?	"OK, I guess"
Entertaining and hosting?	"Not sure"
Staying in touch with people?	"Just OK"

How did you help the firm last year—

Retain business?	"All the clients I worked on are still here"
Cross-sell services?	"Haven't tried"
Add new clients?	"Helping to bring in XYZ client was fun"
Increase the referral base?	"Didn't"
Create a larger awareness of the firm?	"Didn't"

How would you describe the position you want to have within the firm the next three years?

"I want to be a manager within the next two to three years. Beyond that, I am not sure whether I want to be a partner or whether there would even be a chance."

What do you think your chances are of achieving it?

"I think I would be a good manager and I believe that is what the firm wants me to do."

What do you think the firm needs to do to help you?

"Coaching, guidance, suggestions, monetary support, time as per personal marketing plan."

■ ■ ■

Part 2: My Personal Marketing Plan

Based on the above and the Evaluation Tools in chapters 2 and 3, (exhibits 2–2 and 3–1 to 3–6), my personal marketing plan is driven by the following long-term objectives:

1. Become a manager within two years.

2. Develop the specialty of serving clients in the restaurant and manufacturing industries.

In order to make progress toward accomplishing these goals this year, I plan to take the action described:

1. Create a larger awareness of our firm in the restaurant industry.

    a. Ask client XYZ to sponsor me for membership in restaurant association.

    b. Join the association.

    c. Get on the program committee.

2. Demonstrate my understanding of the industry's business and accounting issues.

    a. Identify and research ten industry "hot issues," and use those issues for discussion with industry leaders, and target and current clients.

    b. Write and place one article in an association newsletter or industry publication.

    c. Attend AICPA classes on restaurant financial management.

    d. Present a financial management workshop for the membership with partner Bob.

3. Build my confidence running meetings.

    a. Complete a Dale Carnegie course.

    b. Establish relationships with other students.

    c. Run six committee meetings.

    d. Have a colleague or partner evaluate and give immediate feedback on four meetings I run.

4. Develop a referral relationship with four bankers.

    a. Identify and meet with at least four different bankers of existing clients, two within the restaurant industry.

    b. Learn what the bankers know of our services, whether or not their experience with our firm has been positive, work to further educate them about what we do, and ask for more introductions to their restaurant clients or industry vendors (include partner Bob or manager Lily).

    c. Identify and refer opportunities for new business to these bankers.

5. Develop effective delegation skills.

    a. Attend AICPA or state society classes on delegation.

    b. Present a summary to the staff.

6. *Develop my networking skills to broaden my network of contacts and referral sources.*

    a. Sit with new people at all association meetings.

    b. Write two notes of thanks or acknowledgment weekly.

    c. Identify twenty key associates or contacts or referral sources and "do lunch" with one every week.

    d. Take a class on business manners and social skills.

7. *Add $10,000 of fees from new clients or new services to existing clients.*

    a. Identify six target clients in the restaurant industry and set up information-gathering meetings with each. Tour their facilities. Explore how our firm can be of service.

    b. Learn about our other services, match opportunities with firm expertise, and propose to existing clients.

    c. Monitor progress and report new business.

8. *Establish appropriate timelines for each activity in order to accomplish all within twelve months.*

The support I need is the following:

1. Quarterly meetings with a partner to monitor activity, and get feedback and encouragement

2. Time-budgeted for association activity, meetings with bankers, and training and classes

3. Costs reimbursed for classes, entertainment, and other related expenses

APPENDIX B—PARTNER LEVEL SAMPLE WORKSHEET AND PERSONAL MARKETING PLAN

Part 1: Worksheet for Developing a Personal Marketing Plan at the Partner/Shareholder Level

The purpose of this worksheet is to help the user develop a personal marketing plan that fits his or her current situation, helps the firm retain and grow its client base, and enhances career development. There are a number of questions that need to be answered and from those answers some goals and action should become obvious. The worksheet is best used if the individual is working with a coach or mentor.

Where are you now in your professional development? If your firm has position descriptions which one best describes your current situation?

"I'm a partner and have been for seven years. I'm responsible for client service and handle about $400,000 in billings annually. I'm in charge of our financial reporting department."

What could you be doing that would help those you supervise better serve existing clients?

"Turn over more client responsibility to our managers and develop a program that helps us cull undesirable clients, while spending more time with existing clients and referral sources."

Which industries do you really enjoy?

"Manufacturing and distribution."

In which areas of technical expertise are you an expert?

"Financial statement compliance and reporting, projections, and budgeting."

Are there areas of technical expertise in which you want to be known for your expertise?

"Cash flow management appears to be an area in which a number of our clients do not know what to do. I would like to help more of them become better cash flow managers."

How effective are you at:

Speaking in front of a group? "Pretty good"

Conducting meetings? "Efficient"

Listening? "I think, very good."

Writing? "Don't do much"

Delegation? "Could be better"

Coaching? "Coach four staff now and they're doing fine."

Consensus building? "Don't know"

Selling or persuading? "Do OK"

Personally presenting a
professional image? "I think I do this very well."

Entertaining and hosting? "Do occasionally, feel confident"

Staying in touch with clients
and referral sources? "Only during engagements"

How did you help the firm last year:

Retain business? "Only lost one client, due to a merger."

Cross-sell services? "Sold estate tax project, helped get new computer system in XYZ company."

Add new clients? "Brought in two new clients for financial reporting and tax work."

Increase the referral base? "No new referral sources. Did meet with a couple of bankers."

Create a larger awareness
of the firm? "Not sure I did much. Not as active in trade, professional, and community organizations as I was a few years ago."

How would you describe the position or role you want to have within the firm the next two or three years?

> "Want to be more of a rainmaker and be known in the community as more of a client advocate."

What do you think your chances of achieving it are?

> "Pretty good, I think."

What do you think the firm needs to do to help you?

> "Hold me accountable. Have the managing partner check on me and my plan progress. Give me a manager to do more review of work and have me do more override and final review."

■ ■ ■

Part 2: My Personal Marketing Plan

Based on the above and the Evaluation Tools in chapters 2 and 3 (exhibits 2-2 and 3-1 to 3-6), my personal marketing plan is driven by the following long-term objectives:

1. Develop and implement an effective client retention program that demonstrates continuous improvement in the quality of clients.

2. Increase my rainmaking activities so that my results improve 20 percent each year (based on the $50,000 of new business I developed last year).

In order to do that, I plan to create these results this year by taking the action described:

1. *Develop a client retention program and use it to improve clients or refer them to another CPA firm.*

   a. Establish criteria and a program to evaluate clients against that criteria.

   b. Use this program to improve or drop 10 clients currently below the established criteria.

   c. Explain the program to all partners with the intention of getting them to use it too.

2. *Develop a cash flow management program for wholesale distributors.*

    a. Work with Betty, Executive Director of the Wholesale Distribution Association, to present the program twice during the year to the membership.

    b. Present one luncheon speech about the importance of cash management.

3. *Nurture existing relationships with current referral sources.*

    a. Identify and target two bankers at the Commerce Bank, and two at the Community Bank. Meet with them to explore mutual clients, referral possibilities, and getting business.

    b. Identify and target four lawyers specializing in manufacturing industries. Meet with them to explore mutual clients, referral possibilities, and getting business.

4. *Turn over more client responsibility to managers.*

    a. Invite managers along for all client meetings.

    b. Identify ten clients and shift more client responsibility to managers.

5. *Add $60,000 in billings within twelve months.*

    a. Increase new business activity by $50,000.

    b. Increase services to existing clients by $10,000.

The support I need is the following:

1. Resources to put on cash management seminars, to include staff and partner attendance and follow-through with attendees

2. Manager, Paula, free to do more review work

3. Support to cull or improve these clients: ABC, DEF, GHI, and JKL, and identify and target six more

APPENDIX C—TABLE MANNERS FOR THE BUSINESS PROFESSIONAL

"They don't teach etiquette much anymore, but if you have a chance to choose between Incredibly Advanced Accounting for Overachievers and Remedial Knife and Fork, head for the silverware."

—Harvey Mackay, author, business owner

I have always wondered why people save their best manners for when they are out with strangers, while reserving their less-than-mannerly side for their families, friends, and themselves. If someone has self-respect, then doesn't one deserve to experience the best side of oneself too?

The truth is, most of us want to do things properly. We dread embarrassment. Old habits follow us, even though they can be changed. Our table manners say a lot about us and the way we conduct business. In fact, many a job offer has been rescinded after a business meal. In the corporate world, poor table manners are associated with poor manners in general. The assumption is that if you were taught manners at home, you would have been taught table manners. Today, companies cannot afford to hire socially inept people.

Since dining is an integral part of doing business successfully, it is important to understand that many a sale or career has been short-circuited by a lack of dining etiquette. It is interesting that this subject is the most sought after and talked about in my seminars. It is also the most fun because we can put the information to use immediately and can experience our self-confidence rising. After all, table manners are not complicated. Dining etiquette is not rocket science; it is about eating— something we all do every day.

At the same time, we could go on for pages on the subject of food, eating, dining, and entertaining. If you develop a sense of observation, you'll find that people who appear poised, confident, and sophisticated are able to handle themselves at the table, around food, and while entertaining with grace and style.

John Molloy reported research in his book, *Live for Success*, that underlines the importance of solid dining skills.[21] When the researchers observed the CEOs, presidents, and chairmen-of-the-board of Fortune 500 companies, they found that 80 percent had impeccable table manners. Forty percent of those in middle management and only 12 percent of those right out of school had good table manners. Even more significant was the reaction of management to poor table manners. Over 60 percent of managers said they would not consider letting an employee represent their company publicly unless that person knew how to handle him- or herself at the table. Good table manners are an absolute requirement for any executive in their corporation.

---

[21] John T. Molloy. *Live for Success*. New York: William Morrow and Co., Inc., 1981.

MAKE SURE YOUR TABLE MANNERS ARE NOT OUT TO LUNCH

Whether you like it or not, your table manners can make a difference between getting the job, the promotion, the business, or not getting it. The good news is, we eat every day. This gives us the opportunity to practice our table manners daily. With this kind of attention, you will develop positive habits quickly. And you will therefore feel more confident and comfortable in business, quasi-business, and social settings.

The subject of entertaining, dining, and table manners has filled many books. We will briefly review dining basics here. I encourage you to seek reference books that can teach you more. You will be glad you spent the time and made the effort to increase your dining skills.

The Table Setting

Formal table settings, with all the silverware, may seem intimidating, but only until you understand the system behind it all. Simpler settings, such as one would find on the table for lunch, are variations of the more formal dinner setting.

Placement and Procedure

- Forks will be on your left, knives on your right, with the blades facing inward. Exceptions are:

  —The oyster or seafood fork will be on the right, next to the soup spoon.

  —The dessert fork is above the plate.

  —The butter knife will be on the butter plate.

- Start with the utensils on the outside and work inward with each subsequent course.

- The server will usually remove any unused utensils. For example, the soup spoon will be removed if you do not order soup.

- The teaspoon used for coffee and tea is most often found above your plate with the dessert service, since coffee is served after the meal. Sometimes, at luncheon settings, it will be found to the right of the plate.

- If you do not use a utensil with a course, such as a salad knife, it will be removed by the server when the salad plate and salad fork are removed. Do not place used utensils on your soiled plate.

- A simple rule to remember is this: "Solids to the left, liquids to the right." Since 85 percent of us are right-handed, our glasses and cups are to our right, our butter plate to the left. Knowing this, you will not embarrass yourself by using your neighbor's butter dish for your bread.

- Place utensils on the service plate after eating soup or dessert.

INFORMAL TABLE SETTING

bread knife

dessert spoon

bread plate

dessert fork

water

wine

napkin

fork

knife

spoon

FORMAL TABLE SETTING

champagne

place card

water

bread knife

dessert spoon

red wine

white wine

bread plate

dessert fork

sherry

oyster fork

fish fork

dinner fork

salad fork

menu

napkin

salad knife

dinner knife

fish knife

soup spoon

181

Eating Styles

The two basic eating styles for using utensils are the American (Zigzag) and Continental. The Continental style originated in Europe and is practiced throughout the world (where utensils are used) with variations. Both are accepted and practiced in the United States today.

With the Continental style, the knife is held in the right hand (the predominant hand) throughout the main courses, with the fork in the left. They are held exactly the way the knife and fork are held in the American style when cutting food—the handles in the palm of the hands, tines down.

In the American style, the knife is in the predominant hand only when cutting food, then it is placed across the top of the plate, and the fork is switched from the left hand to the right for eating. When you need to cut another piece, the fork is switched back to the left hand, the knife is picked up, one to two pieces are cut, and the process starts over—thus the zigzag tag.

The main problem observed at the table is that of incorrectly holding the utensils. Too many people today do not know how to hold the fork and knife properly while cutting. This is a dead giveaway that they have not been taught table manners. Remember, rules of etiquette are based in part on efficiency. Therefore, to cut food efficiently, the knife and fork are held with the handles in the palm of the hand, the index fingers on top, and the other fingers wrapped around the handles. The knife and fork are held nearly parallel to the table.

Many people mistakenly hold the fork almost perpendicular to the table with finger tips holding the handle. It is an inefficient way to hold something in place on your plate and it is incorrect. Observe others in fine restaurants and watch how they hold their utensils, and start practicing at home to develop positive habits that are the mark of a well-mannered person.

Keep in mind the following.

- Since the dinner knife is not serrated, it cuts in one direction. Draw the knife toward you, lift it, and draw it toward you again.
- Serrated knives, such as steak knives, do cut in both directions, so a back and forth motion is appropriate.
- Leave your butter knife on the butter plate when not in use. If no butter knife is provided, use your dinner knife.
- Never rest utensils half on and half off the china.
- Do not use your finger as a pusher. Use your knife.
- At the end of a meal, place only the utensils you have used on the plate.
- Do not push your plate away when finished.

■ The following illustration shows the "silent signals" to the serving staff that indicate whether or not you are finished. This helps the staff be efficient but not intrusive.

 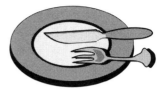

To indicate you are finished
(when only a fork was used)

To indicate you are finished
(when both a knife and fork were used)

■ Remember that Thais eat with a spoon and fork in their hands throughout the meal, not chopsticks.

■ Only 45 percent of the world eat with a knife, fork, and spoon; 36 percent eat with chopsticks. If you are involved with international clients, learn to use chopsticks properly.

At the Table

The following are some tips on how to correctly approach and leave the table, as well as how to seat yourself at the table.

■ Place purses, briefcases, and all other personal items at your feet or under your chair so that these items are out of the way of servers, who will need room to serve from the left and clear from the right. Purses and briefcases should not be placed on the table.

■ Push your chair back before leaving the table.

■ Never put your elbows on the table. The exception is between courses, when you may do so only in order to help you lean forward to hear better. Always keep your elbows close to your sides.

■ You may rest your forearms, near the wrist and without leaning on them, on the table.

■ Sit upright at the table with your feet comfortably on the floor. Lean forward to meet your lifted fork without dropping your head.

■ Never rock on a chair when seated at the table.

The following are suggestions for the correct use of table napkins.

- Remove your napkin from the table, only after everyone is seated, but before orders are taken.

- To unfold your napkin, hold to your side, and shake gently.

- Leave a large napkin folded in half, and place it on your lap with the fold toward you.

- Blot your mouth or lips with the napkin before taking a drink from a glass or cup.

- If you leave the table in the middle of the meal, place your napkin on the chair, either its seat, arm, or back. (This is one of the silent signals to the staff that you will be back.)

- Keep your napkin on your lap until you leave the table.

- At the end of the meal, when you are ready to leave the table, place the napkin to the left of your plate. Never leave your napkin—even if it is a paper napkin—on top of your plate.

When passing foods at the table, remember the following.

- If the bread basket, butter, or salad dressing is in front of you, don't wait to be asked, take some then pass it to your right.

- After the items have been passed initially, they don't have to continue being passed to the right. The person nearest the item would pass it to the person requesting it.

- Always pass the salt and pepper together; never separate them.

- When you pass anything with a handle, such as a creamer, salad dressing boat, or coffee decanter, the handle should be turned toward the person receiving it.

If you have trouble eating a certain food or foods, avoid them when you are out for business. Avoid messy foods and those that can cause embarrassment. Practice in the privacy of your home and with friends, not while out for business. Remember the following particulars about food.

- Tear rather than cut bread or rolls. Butter only a bite or two, not the entire slice.

- Crisp bacon is finger food. Cut bacon that isn't crisp.

- Never wash down food with a liquid. Clear your mouth first.

- You may tip your cup of soup away from you to get the last of it. Move your spoon away from you as well, to scoop the soup.

- Don't crumble and drop crackers into your soup. Oysterettes and small fish crackers can be dropped in the soup—but not all at once.

- If you must cut salad greens, try to do so with the edge of the fork first. If this doesn't work well, then use your knife, cutting only a few bites.

- Although North Americans tend to prefer to use a large spoon to assist them in eating long pasta, Italians do not favor this technique. It is considered incorrect to cut long pasta. If you must cut your pasta, cut only a bite or two at a time.

■ Unless you are dining at a ribs joint or with the Colonel, don't pick up your chicken or chops or chew meat off a bone. Learn to use a knife and fork effectively.

The following are examples of potentially awkward moments and how to avoid them.

■ Cherry tomatoes can cause a scene. If you cut one in half, be careful. The juice, seeds, and the tomato itself can fly great distances. If you eat it whole, make sure it's not too big.

■ Remove fish bones from your mouth with your fingers. All other inedibles, however, such as gristle or cartilage, should be rolled forward in the mouth, pushed onto your fork, placed on your dinner plate, and then covered with something, like a garnish, if possible.

■ Sneeze or cough into a handkerchief. A napkin may be used to block a sneeze, but never blow your nose into a napkin, even if it's paper.

■ Acknowledge burps with a softly spoken "excuse me," to no one in particular.

■ Excuse yourself from the table to handle something caught in your teeth, a coughing attack, or to blow your nose.

■ Never use a toothpick at the table.

■ Most people are offended by grooming in public. Apply makeup in the powder room, if you must.

The following are additional basics.

■ Chew food with your mouth closed.

■ Don't talk with your mouth full of food.

■ Don't blow on hot food or drinks. Stir the hot food or let it sit awhile.

■ Don't use bread for a pusher or for dunking. To enjoy the last of a sauce, drop a piece of bread on your plate, and retrieve it with your fork.

■ Don't wave or gesture with utensils in your hand.

■ Ask to have things passed. Never reach if the food isn't directly in front of you.

■ Don't cut up an entire piece of meat, pancake, or any other foods, at once. Cut between one and three bites only.

■ Don't hand your plate to the server as they attempt to clear the table.

■ Don't leave lipstick marks on cups and glasses. It's a huge turnoff. Blot lips well before eating.

■ Include everyone in the conversation.

■ Don't dominate the conversation.

■ Keep your voice down, which is a good practice in all public places.

■ Pace your eating to conform to the pace of the others present. It is acceptable to leave food on your plate, and it is also acceptable to eat everything. It is the timing that counts.

- Don't gulp and shovel food into your mouth as if you were eating your last meal.

- Don't read at the table if you have guests. (This may seem very obvious, but it is one of the commonly cited reasons why firms request etiquette training. Even partners get too comfortable with longtime clients and forget their manners!)

Cocktail Functions

Cocktail functions are a special category of event with a few rules of their own. Above all, cocktails are not a meal. Bear in mind that you are there for the business and the conversation, not the food. The following are pointers to remember at these events, where you will eat lightly.

- Never eat something directly from a serving plate.

- Don't double dip (dip a chip, take a bite, redip, and eat).

- Do not try to eat and drink at the same time unless you are able to sit at a table. If you are standing, balancing a drink in one hand, and appetizers in the other becomes very awkward, and greeting and shaking hands becomes impossible.

- Avoid messy foods. Greasy or sticky fingers will make a terrible impression on anyone you shake hands with, or will inhibit you from shaking hands at all. Also note that licking your fingers is tempting but unacceptable behavior.

- Take small bites of food and sips that do not interrupt or distract from your conversation.

You can see that the possession of certain social skills, dining and table manners, is a prerequisite to success in the business world. And remember, your table manners are a gift you give those with whom you dine. Bon appetit!

SUGGESTED READING AND RESOURCES FOR YOUR FIRM LIBRARY

BUSINESS MANNERS AND ETIQUETTE

Baldrige, Letitia. *Letitia Baldrige's Complete Guide To The New Manners for the '90s.* New York: Rawson Associates, 1990.

Baldrige, Letitia. *Letitia Baldrige's New Complete Guide to Executive Manners.* New York: Rawson Associates, 1993.

Dunckel, Jacqueline. *Business Etiquette Today.* Vancouver, BC: Self-Counsel Press, 1987.

Klinkenberg, Hilka. *At Ease...Professionally.* Chicago: Bonus Books, 1992.

Pachter, Barbara and Marjorie Brody. *Complete Business Etiquette Handbook.* New York: Prentice Hall, 1995.

Post, Elizabeth. *Emily Post's Advice for Every Dining Occasion.* New York: HarperCollins Publishers, 1994.

Sabath, Ann Marie. *Business Etiquette in Brief.* Holbrook, MA: Bob Adams, Inc., 1993.

CAREER DEVELOPMENT

Kanter, Rosabeth Moss. *When Giants Learn to Dance: Mastering the Challenge of Strategy, Management, and Careers in the 1990s.* New York: Simon & Schuster, 1990.

Mackay, Harvey. *Shark Proof: Get the Job You Want, Keep the Job You Love... In Today's Frenzied Job Market.* New York: Harper Business, 1993.

Ryan, Robin. *60 Seconds & You're Hired!* Manassas Park, VA: Impact Publications, 1994.

COMMUNICATION SKILLS

Elsea, Janet, Ph.D. *First Impression, Best Impression.* New York: Simon & Schuster, 1985.

Peoples, David. *Presentations Plus.* New York: John Wiley & Sons, 1988.

Van Fleet, James. *Conversational Power.* Englewood Cliffs, NJ: Prentice-Hall, 1984.

Walther, George. *Power Talking.* New York: G.P. Putnam's Sons, 1991.

CUSTOMER/CLIENT SERVICE

Alessandra, Tony, Ph.D. and Michael J. O'Connor, Ph.D. *The Platinum Rule.* New York: Warner Books, Inc., 1996.

Rosenbluth, Hal and Diane McFerrin Peters. *The Customer Comes Second.* New York: William Morrow, 1992.

Sewell, Carl and Paul Brown. *Customers for Life.* New York: Doubleday Currency, 1990.

Spector, Robert and Patrick McCarthy. *The Nordstrom Way.* New York: John Wiley & Sons, 1995.

Willingham, Ron. *Hey, I'm The Customer.* Englewood Cliffs, NJ: Prentice Hall, 1992.

GENERAL BUSINESS

Harvey, Eric and Alexander Lucia. *Walk The Talk...And Get the Results You Want.* Dallas: Performance Publishers, 1995.

Thiederman, Sondra, Ph.D. *Profiting in America's Multicultural Marketplace.* New York: Lexington Books, 1991.

GLOBAL BUSINESS

Chesanow, Neil. *The World-Class Executive.* New York: Bantam Books, 1985.

Copeland, Lennie and Lewis Griggs. *Going International.* New York: Random House, 1985.

Engholm, Christopher. *When Business East Meets Business West.* New York: John Wiley & Sons, 1991.

Engholm, Christopher. *Doing Business in Asia's Booming "China Triangle."* Englewood Cliffs, NJ: Prentice Hall, 1994.

Snowdon, Sondra. *The Global Edge.* New York: Simon & Schuster, 1986.

INTERNATIONAL ETIQUETTE

Axtell, Roger. *Do's and Taboos of Hosting International Visitors.* New York: John Wiley & Sons, 1989.

Axtell, Roger. *Gestures: The Do's and Taboos of Body Language Around the World.* New York: John Wiley & Sons, 1991.

Bosrock, Mary Murray. *Put Your Best Foot Forward: Asia.* St. Paul, MN: IES, 1994.

Bosrock, Mary Murray. *Put Your Best Foot Forward: Europe.* St. Paul, MN: IES, 1994.

Bosrock, Mary Murray. *Put Your Best Foot Forward: Mexico/Canada.* St. Paul MN: IES, 1995.

De Mente, Boye. *Chinese Etiquette and Ethics in Business.* Lincolnwood, IL: NTC Business Books, 1995.

De Mente, Boye. *Japanese Etiquette and Ethics in Business.* Lincolnwood, IL: NTC Business Books, 1993.

De Mente, Boye. *Korean Etiquette and Ethics in Business.* Lincolnwood, IL: NTC Business Books, 1994.

Morrison, Terri, Wayne Conaway, and George Borden, Ph.D. *Kiss, Bow, or Shake Hands: How To Do Business in Sixty Countries.* Holbrook, MA: Bob Adams, Inc., 1994.

The Parker Pen Company. *Do's and Taboos Around the World.* New York: The Benjamin Company, 1985.

Richmond, Yale. *From Da to Yes: Understanding the East Europeans.* Yarmouth, ME: Intercultural Press, 1995.

MANAGEMENT

Covey, Stephen. *Principle-Centered Leadership.* New York: Summit Books, 1991.

Jellison, Jerald. *Overcoming Resistance: A Practical Guide to Producing Change in the Workplace.* New York: Simon and Schuster, 1993.

LeBoeuf, Michael, Ph.D. *The Greatest Management Principle in the World.* New York: Berkley Books, 1985.

Sonnenberg, Frank. *Managing With a Conscience.* New York: McGraw-Hill, Inc., 1994.

MARKETING

Connor, Dick and Jeffrey Davidson. *Marketing Your Consulting and Professional Services.* New York: John Wiley & Sons, Inc., 1990.

Nassuti, Colette, ed. *The Marketing Advantage.* New York: AICPA, 1994.

MOTIVATION AND INSPIRATION

Nightingale, Earl. *The Essence of Success.* Niles, IL: Nightingale-Conant Corp., 1993.

Peale, Dr. Norman Vincent. *The Power of Positive Living.* New York: Doubleday, 1990.

NETWORKING

Baker, Wayne E. *Networking Smart.* New York: McGraw-Hill, Inc., 1994.

Baber, Anne and Lynne Waymon. *Great Connections.* Manassas Park, VA: Impact Productions, 1992.

Burg, Bob. *Endless Referrals.* New York: McGraw-Hill, Inc., 1994.

RoAne, Susan. *How to Work a Room.* New York: Shapolshy Publishers, Inc., 1988.

RoAne, Susan. *The Secrets of Savvy Networking.* New York: Warner Books, 1993.

PERSONAL EFFECTIVENESS

Covey, Stephen. *The Seven Habits of Highly Effective People.* New York: Simon & Schuster, 1989.

Fisher, Roger and Scott Brown. *Getting Together: Building Relationships as We Negotiate.* New York: Penguin Books, 1988.

Helmstetter, Shad, Ph.D. *What to Say When You Talk to Yourself.* New York: Pocket Books, 1986.

Klauser, Henriette Anne. *Writing on Both Sides of the Brain.* San Francisco: Harper & Row, 1986.

Sabin, William. *The Gregg Reference Manual,* Sixth Edition. New York: McGraw-Hill, Inc., 1991.

Strunk, Jr., William and E.B. White. *The Elements of Style,* Third Edition. New York: McMillan, 1979.

PROFESSIONAL PRESENCE

Bixler, Susan. *Professional Presence.* New York: G.P. Putnam's Sons, 1991.

SELLING

Brennan, Jr., Charles D. *Sales Questions That Close the Sale: How to Uncover Your Customers' Real Needs.* New York: AMACOM, 1994.

Peoples, David. *Selling to the Top.* New York: John Wiley & Sons, 1993.

Rackham, Neil. *Spin Selling.* New York: McGraw-Hill, Inc., 1988.

VALUES, VIRTUES, AND ETHICS

Bennett, William. *The Book of Virtues.* New York: Simon & Schuster, 1993.

Blanchard, Kenneth, Ph.D., and Dr. Norman Vincent Peale. *The Power of Ethical Management.* New York: Ballantine Books, 1988.

Dosick, Wayne. *Golden Rules: The Ten Ethical Values Parents Need to Teach Their Children.* New York: HarperCollins Publishers, 1995.

ABOUT THE AUTHOR

Randi is a graduate of the University of Washington in Home Economics and is certified in family and consumer sciences. She has been training and public speaking throughout North America since 1970 and has owned her Seattle-based company since 1977. She brings experience and knowledge to her audiences with wit, warmth, and understanding. Her focus over the last fifteen years has been in helping people build and nurture long-term business relationships through solid interpersonal communication and the social skills that are critical for building a solid client base and a rewarding career.

Randi is well known throughout the accounting industry in the United States and Canada. She has presented keynotes, speeches, and workshops for the AICPA, CGA of Canada, many state societies, the Big Six, regional and local accounting firms, as well as partner retreats and those involved in groups such as The American Group of CPA Firms. Price Waterhouse featured her in an in-house training film. She has authored many articles for national publications.

Although her focus has been the accounting and consulting fields, other clients include Boeing Commercial Airline Group, Andersen Consulting, Nordstrom, Alaska Airlines, Port of Seattle, Bank of America, Westin Hotels and Resorts, National Park Service, the United States Department of Labor, and many national associations. She is also a regular guest instructor at several universities, helping graduate students with their personal marketing skills.